WOMEN WINNING

A Handbook for Action
against
Sex Discrimination

WOMEN WINNING

A Handbook for Action against Sex Discrimination

Virginia E. Pendergrass,
Editor

Nelson-Hall nh Chicago

Library of Congress Cataloging in Publication Data

Main entry under title:

Women winning.

    Bibliography: p.
    Includes index.
    1. Women—Employment—United States—Case studies.
2. Sex discrimination against women—United States—
case studies. 3. Discrimination in employment—United
States—Case studies. I. Pendergrass, Virginia E.
HD6095.W697   331.1′33   78-27379
ISBN 0-88229-450-4 (Cloth)
ISBN 0-88229-699-X (Paper)

Manufactured in the United States of America

10   9   8   7   6   5   4   3   2   1

Contents

1

Introduction[*]

Virginia E. Pendergrass

In 1964, Congress passed the Civil Rights Act which prohibited discrimination in employment on the basis of race, color, religion, national origin, or sex. The provision relating to sex was added in an attempt to sabotage the passage of the Civil Rights Act by making it appear ridiculous to Congress. Women didn't laugh; they filed approximately 15,000 charges with the Equal Employment Opportunity Commission (EEOC) during its first five and one-half years. Unfortunately, the EEOC did not have the power to enforce findings of sex discrimination. Only about 50 percent of the complaints found justified by EEOC were successfully resolved.[1] This means that many, many women went through the difficult process of filing a just claim, with all the ensuing harassment, time and anxiety, and still received nothing in return. A few especially courageous (or outraged) women went on to file private legal suits which cost hundreds of dollars and days.

---

[*]Portions of this book were previously published in V.E. Pendergrass, E. Kimmel, J. Joesting, J. Petersen, and E. Bush, "Sex Discrimination Counseling," *American Psychologist* 31 (1976): 36–46.

Numerous commissions were formed to report on sex discrimination and take action to improve the status of women. Academic women carefully documented discrimination in hiring[2,3,4], pay and promotion[5,6] and performance of work duties[7,8], even though women were and are as well-qualified as men.[9,10,11,12,13]

Nothing changed. Even when new legislation empowered EEOC to take action in federal courts when voluntary compliance failed[14] we cannot say that sex discrimination has been substantially reduced. Four years after the Civil Rights Act became law, full-time women workers still earned only 58 percent of what fully employed men workers earned.[15] Differences appear to have *increased* since then, *not* disappeared.[16,17]

Feeling is mounting that progress will be made only through direct, vigorous protest on a day-in, day-out basis. This more militant stance of women, however, is generating the traditional backlash.[18]

In an attempt to support and encourage women involved in challenging entrenched sex discrimination, the American Psychological Association invited regional associations to present workshops on this topic. Some of the papers in this book grew out of a workshop sponsored by the Southeastern Psychological Association Commission for the Status of Women in 1974.

Chairs of programs and other university officers in influential positions were invited to participate. Unfortunately, the meeting was attended primarily by women who faced sex discrimination and who were wondering how to handle it. Subsequent meetings at psychological conventions and at other professional meetings have not been successful in enlisting the aid and interest of those whose decisions could bring about rapid change. It's up to women themselves to eradicate sex discrimination. This book is written by women about women who have tried to attack sex discrimination in their own places of employment.

The case herstories and strategical approaches are provided by professional women. We do not directly address the uneducated, poor women whose overwhelming problems with our sexist society stem from conditions of birth, home environment, and education long before adult employment. I think, however, that many of us will be more sensitive to the plight of other women; we ourselves have seen first-hand flagrant and subtle acts of discrimination, experienced anxieties about job security and relationships with others, and borne some of the hostility of those who do not want change.

But we have also seen women winning.

2

Friendly Little Chats

Ellen Kimmel
University of South Florida
Tampa, Florida

In the best of all possible worlds, one should be able to solve life's problems, including sex discrimination in employment, by means of a friendly little chat. At least it's worth a try.

Athena Theodore[1] surveyed 65 women in the process, of protesting sex discrimination. These cases were obtained from answers to questionnaires sent to a larger group of academic women known to be active in the women's movement. Theodore identified four responses of women in seeking remedy for grievances: 1) sensitizing or consciousness-raising; 2) seeking redress through institutional procedures; 3) seeking redress through government agencies, courts, and other outside groups; and 4) working off-campus in the women's movement.

The friendly little chat is an informal, inside activity engaged in by women prior to appeals through formal grievance procedures, union representation, or outside agencies such as the courts, HEW, or EEOC. The period of time required for the chats may be weeks, months, or

5

possibly years, during which endless exchanges of communication—oral, written, and taped—will probably occur as documents pass back and forth and increase in
volume. A friendly little chat is consciousness-raising,
with perhaps a hint of action in reserve.

RECOGNITION OF THE PROBLEM AND
DECISION TO ACT

A preliminary stage in the protest process not discussed at any length by Theodore[2] is the dawning recognition of the problem by the woman herself. Although a
woman may have suffered sex discrimination for years,
she is likely to be unaware of any difficulty in employment and/or of its source in her membership in the 51 percent minority.[3] Since women as a group learn to devalue
their own talents and accomplishments,[4][5][6] realization of
discrimination is often slow in coming.

Even after a woman becomes "conscious," she may not
act. Women are trained not to rock the boat. A specific
incident may have to occur before anger is finally sparked;
an unexpected termination notice, rejection for a position,
failure to be promoted, low salary or low raise, a capricious rule change, denial of a chance to teach a preferred
course, or being asked to serve refreshments one time too
many may provoke her into action. More often, a woman
decides to fight back after she comes to the terrible
recognition that she has nothing to lose.

In most instances, she has made every effort to secure
equality through hard work and demonstrated competence, and in the end concludes that it has been, and will
continue to be, of no avail. Thus, the protest results from a
combination of sensitization to the problem and discovery
that justice cannot be achieved by good performance. By
the time awareness develops and sufficient anger is
aroused, a large number of inequalities may have accumu-
lated. Because only one of a host of problems may be
identified at first, her case will become increasingly complex as the others gradually come to light.

For women or counselors of women who are considering action of some sort, a caveat or two are in order. First,
any particular woman's situation can safely be assumed

to be an integral part of institutionalized patterns of sexist employment practices. For a complete description of institutionalization of sexism in industry, see Copus et al.[7] It would be a naive hope that a conversation with a single, just man (I use the sex advisedly) would serve to undo an injustice which is standard operating procedure. Furthermore, it would be naive to assume that one can scientifically pick the right moment or person to broach the issue, or know whether or not to carry a big stick (or try to use it). In other words, each woman or group of women will travel an uncharted path, and there are no guarantees. In my first experience with the friendly little chat, I failed to get an answer from my department head regarding the amount of a raise. I hounded the business manager until he gave up the information; the figure was a laughable $60 for two years. I immediately went to the Dean with whom I had a beautiful **friendly** little chat and from whom I received wonderful promises of relief. What I actually received three months later was a letter of non-renewal of my employment contract.

The Department of Health, Education and Welfare and other government agencies, as well as the courts, strongly urge a complainant to exhaust all possible means of redress within the system before outside action is taken. Thus, the friendly little chat is a necessary evil.

PREPARATION

Data collection is going to be an integral part of the protesting woman's existence. All the facts about her case should be collected and organized as carefully and as accurately as possible. The appearance of reports and other information which document sex discrimination in the institution or agency is very important because it may serve to raise the consciousness of the administrators who will ultimately decide the woman's fate. The greater the number of women who can be shown to suffer sex discrimination, the greater the chances are to convince the powers that be that sex discrimination is a problem. The first response of the typical administrator to information about a woman's case is, at best, that her problems are either due to an "oversight" or to the woman's own peculiar personality. Unfortunately, even when administrators are convinced that sex discrimination does exist, generally they still decline to admit that a specific instance falls in that category.

In addition to data collection, the woman should find some friends to support her publicly. The best friends are those who are sympathetic, agree there is sex bias, and *have no employment problems themselves* at present. Friends with strong credentials and established reputations can ward off her feelings that she is wrong, and these friends can appear objective to others in arguing this as a case of sex discrimination.

Once a woman points her finger, she must be prepared factually and psychologically for retaliation. The woman must rehearse how she is going to behave. She must steel herself to maintain her composure while being insulted, ignored, patronized, cross-examined, or dressed down. In any event, she must strive *not* to provide the institutuion with ammunition by responding emotionally, unfair as that may be. The woman must think in terms of gathering ammunition from the emotional responses of institutional representatives.

TAKING ACTION: THE CHAT IS HELD

In most instances, the first chat is held with a department head or the immediately responsible administrator. After this, the individuals and groups with whom the woman must deal vary from place to place. Seldom is the first chat the last. She will probably find herself repeating over and over the well-documented information to various persons, committees, and administrators up to and including the president of the organization.

Not infrequently, the process of having friendly little chats results in the development of an adversary relationship. This is why it is very important that the tone and content of discussions be controlled and deliberate. It cannot be urged too strongly that the woman make some kind of record of each conversation. Tape recordings, the best record, lead to a more formal kind of interaction. The next best is the presence of a witness. If neither is possible, the woman must sit down immediately after the conversation and write out everything she remembers. This means that she will have only her word against his, but careful, daily records may be useful when a more formal action is contemplated. Such daily recordings may be read into a court record. A woman may improve her legal and nonlegal status to some extent by sending a memo summarizing the interaction to the other party, to establish some tangible record. It will be particularly useful if the content of the memo is not challenged by the recipient.

Since the woman who is being exploited is often a second-class citizen, she must plead from a weak position. She may not enjoy equal participation in departmental discussions and decision-making. She may have little to say about her work load. She has to expect subtle kinds of harassment, difficult to document, which impede her pursuit of the case. The more she presses, the more her appeals may fall into bureaucratic quicksand. One of the reasons she may find herself talking herself to death is that many institutions, lacking established grievance machinery, may create machinery as fast as the woman exhausts it.

THE INSTITUTION'S RESPONSE

Perhaps the institution, apprised of the injustice, will move quickly to rectify it. If so, give thanks and be generous in praising those responsible. Sometimes a woman is lucky, and it is admitted that an "oversight" has occurred. However, resistance in various forms is more apt to be the institutional reaction to friendly little chats.

Women face female stereotypes which are thrown at them as they venture to question the authoritative judgment of male superiors. In saying that her problem is due to personality conflict, not sexism, administrators or colleagues label the woman as too sensitive, over-reacting, or just plain difficult. See Bird[8] for a discussion of sex-role expectations in the business world.

A second line of resistance women will encounter is secrecy, often disguised as confidentiality. This renders her especially powerless to respond or take action on her own behalf. It begins when the novice tries to get into the system by applying for a job. Her folder, closed to her, may contain letters of referral which warn the institution of some of her personality characteristics. Such character assassination evidently is not so uncommon as one might think. The employed woman often cannot belong to the very committees who decide her fate and therefore may not be familiar with their operations. She may be forced to utilize grievance procedures which are conducted in secret and she may simply be informed of the "regretful" conclusions, without explanation.

Perhaps the most frustrating of all institutional reactions is delay. The woman's case bounces from department head to administrator, personnel office, committees, affirmative action officers, back to committees and so on. Sometimes the woman is counseled to wait until the affirmative action plan is completed, or revised, or accepted, in order that proper grievance avenues are followed. She may be told that a sex discrimination study is under way and she should wait until its completion—wait for the computer to run; wait for the return of an administrator; or the absence of an administrator; *ad infinitum.*

Yet another ploy which protesting women can anticipate is an attempt to seperate women from each other or to pit the sexes against one another. White men who apply for positions and who are rejected for whatever reason are all too often told that the institution had to hire a black man or a woman. This is an easy way to say no and puts the onus of rejection on unsuspecting women and blacks. Other strategies include rewarding or otherwise manipulating certain women in order to get them to turn against the woman (or women) demanding remedy. Administrators may insinuate that the misbehaving woman is basically incompetent, which leads other women to fear being associated with her cause. It is difficult to judge competence, even among peers. It is easy for authorities to convince people whose own position is vulnerable of the incompetence of someone in a different specialty from their own.

Not to be overlooked in the list of possible institutional responses are outright lying, distortions of truth, omission of information and misleading statements—routine from some administrators. The woman also may simply be ignored. If all else fails to stop a woman from pursuing her cause, the institution may resort to covert or overt intimidation, although this is illegal [9]

COUNTERMOVES

There are several follow-up measures to conteract institutional resistance, sometimes successful and sometimes not. One of the typical responses of women to an unsatisfactory answer to a complaint is to begin or to continue to perform as "superwomen," by out-thinking, out-working, and out-producing all colleagues so that it becomes increasingly difficult for the administration to claim personality problems or incompetence. This is the slowest and least probable of all tactics, since there are limited numbers of superpeople.

Another approach is political action whereby groups of women or interested people join together to fight for the woman's cause, even to the point of demonstrating. Letters to local newsletters and newspapers exposing the problem and the woman's inability to gain a solution through "chatting" channels may help. If widespread adverse publicity or threat of publicity can be accomplished, this may be a potent weapon. The media can be the makers of right.

Providing data and more data to show that the woman's problem is not an isolated example comprises another strategem. Finally, notice of intention to sue or file a formal complaint with an outside group, never to be given unless serious, may yield results.

SUCCESS AND FAILURE

In the fantastic event of success resulting from either a friendly little chat or countermoves, don't forget the power of positive reinforcement. Make certain that those who instituted or pushed for the change and the institution itself get positive publicity for doing the right thing.

This places them in a gentle trap of committing themselves to similar action on future occasions.

In the event of failure, the woman can either drop the complaint and go back to her "place," if she still has one, or embark on the next stages: formal grievances and legal suits.

3

A Case Herstory: An Informal Approach

Anonymous

After my three children reached school age, I wanted to get a college education. I took courses mostly in psychology, because I had in mind going for a master's degree in psychology. Later, however, when I talked to one of the psychology professors, he told me that the program would have no interest in me because I was a woman and I only wanted a master's degree. The school preferred men, particularly those who sought Ph.Ds. I must have had a little yellow in my spine because I just transferred to another school and took a bachelor's degree in sociology (I later entered a master's degree program in public administration).

After graduation, I applied for a substitute teaching certificate, naturally, and at the same time, took every local civil service examination for which I was qualified. I passed all of the exams, and after teaching part-time for a while, the personnel offices called me and/or sent me job opportunity announcements. I got a job as assistant to a program coordinator. The program coordinator was a woman, the only woman in administration of this particular governmental body, and she especially wanted a woman as her assistant. Interestingly, though, when she interviewed me she asked questions like "Do you plan to have any more children?" and "Do you mind working for a woman?"

I was very timid at first, but after a while I wanted more authority and challenge. She did not delegate much, and I felt boxed in. I told her how I felt, and she was very honest with me. She said that I would not get much more responsibility with her, so I knew things would not change.

I didn't want to bounce around from job to job, so I took some time to find out about other opportunities in the same administration. There was a new program developing which called for an assistant to the director. I applied for that job and got it. This seemed a profitable step, because the pay was higher and the job more senior. It was also a new area and would be more challenging. After a time, the program was reorganized and my role was abolished. A new assistant director's position was created. I naturally indicated my interest, but was told that it was usual for such a job to be filled by a man, and that there were other important things which needed to be done. I was assigned to research.

I shared an office with a very intelligent, sympathetic young man who directed the research unit. Although I was not an administrator in the program, I was included in all policy-making conferences. Whenever I said something in these conferences, which I was just beginning to be able to do, I was treated as if I didn't exist, as if I were invisible. It was a terrible experience. When I pointed this out to the unit director, he was very surprised, but started to notice it too. He made a point of recognizing any contributions I made, sometimes favorably and sometimes critically, but at least I knew someone heard me. The other men considered this very amusing or annoying. This young man also pointed out that he had experienced some of the same kind of discrimination because he was young and intelligent (even intelligence can be a disadvantage if it threatens people), which was true.

When the director of this program left, another man was hired. I asked for more challenge, more responsibility, and a better salary. He told me that I was too valuable where I was, and that a supervisory role was out because women did not like to be supervised by women. I told him very calmly that I was going to look for a new position, so that he wouldn't hear of it behind his back.

During this time, a few women urged a lawsuit and I considered it, but I did not want to generate the conflict which it would entail. I also did not want to be forced into a position where everyone would resent and resist me. Nevertheless, the women were very supportive, and helped me by suggesting key words to use in conversations with people and by being available to talk through my frustrations.

There were two men in the overall government administration who hired for special projects. Both were sympathetic to my plight, but one in particular had hired women for other responsible positions—directors and other key roles—and overall displayed a real sense of fairness in dealing with people.

I was due for an increase in pay in my old position, but the budget office held up the increase for over two years. This man was disgusted by the attitude of the budget office and was a very strong advocate for me. I told both of them I was going to hound them until they found something for me. I dropped by periodically and asked "What's up? When will it be?"

Finally, an opening as research analyst on a new project appeared, and I transferred, still with no pay raise and no promotion, but with the possibility of more responsibility and advancement. The project director was a woman. She relied on me for assistance in many important ways. When she left, I was appointed acting director while recruiting took place. The administration wanted a person with special training I did not have. Eventually, however, they conceded that they could not locate the appropriate individual in what was then a critical period for the project, so they appointed me permanent director.

The appointment *and* a substantial raise were announced at a luncheon honoring the newly hired affirmative action director. It took me six years to arrive at a salary of $21,000 and a director's position, which sounds good, but I wonder how that compares with the men here in similar positions.

One of the things that was very helpful to me during this time was an invitation to appear on a professional association's panel on sex discrimination. I did some research on the status of women in government throughout the community and learned a lot about other women. Sex discrimination was and still is a very pervasive problem. There have been a number of women hired or promoted in the last few years, but mostly because of fear of the consequences. Covert attitudes have not changed very much.

I think the thing that was effective about my campaign was the light, pleasant, but very persistent way in which I went about approaching people. If a woman remains courteous and respects individuals, but looks at people "eyeball to eyeball," the basis for her disagreement with people will speak for itself. A woman's case can get lost in the emotional reaction if she resorts to insults and clichés like "male chauvinist pig." Some women who have assaulted the local government were so strident that I would have found them obnoxious myself if we had argued over a grocery cart in the supermarket. When people get angry, doors and minds close.

I used to have more of a tendency to let things go uncorrected, but now I will stand up for what I believe is right all the way to the top, if necessary, and have done it on occasion. In disciplining employees, or in other situations, I always try to give advice in humanly, comfortable, supportive ways.

4

A Case Herstory:
A Business of Her Own

Mary Chichester Dunetz
Conceptual Planning Associates
Coral Gables, Florida

Editor's note: There is much emphasis on "assertive behavior" for women these days. The following case herstory illustrates a constructive use of retreat, the woman who leaves to start her own business. In situations where the system is powerful and nonresponsive or the woman's personality not suited to conflict, this may be the most rational approach to combating sex discrimination.

A few years ago my husband and I separated, expecting to divorce. I realized I would have new, major responsibilities including meeting at least some of my own and my sons' financial needs—a prospect which had a chilling aspect because, although I had worked throughout the marriage, my income had been minor league.

My advertising/public relations experience was great: 17 years of it. But the Miami advertising market was a constantly shifting, unstable one, and my current partnership in an advertising agency did not show any promise of delivering a breadwinner's income.

17

At a local woman's meeting that fall, a young woman introduced herself to the group saying, "I'm new in Miami and I need a job." That inspired me to share my situation with the others: "I'm Mary, I've been here for years and *I* need a job."

A few days later, a friend from that meeting introduced me to a veteran insurance agent who recruited me as his "first woman agent."

The field interested me because I wanted to learn more about business and how money works. And the field was male-dominated, which portended higher incomes. The idea of working only for insurance commissions scared me, but then I had been doing that, in a way, in my own business for five years. And my new general agent said he had no doubt I *could* make a lot of money.

I believe it's important that I mention what seemed to be this general agent's reason for "hiring" me. He was replacing one token with another. The year or so before we met, he had recruited a token Latin male agent. The man had done very well. Too well. He had disappeared, only to reappear on the front pages of the newspaper after being arrested by the police.

The hidden agenda for my becoming an agent was to erase the highly unsatisfactory previous experiment. This didn't faze me, for I felt I certainly wouldn't disgrace my general agent as the previous token had done, and since he had such a vested interest in proving a token could make it, he might give me special training, making it easier for me to master this complex, foreign field.

I was a trainee at the local office. The job itself required that I learn the products (individual life and health policies); exercise my good math ability to learn how to perform multistep calculations on varied policies based on age, sex, occupation, etc; and be able to convince someone to buy. I did learn the products in the rate book; I mastered the various forms and paperflow; I learned how to prepare and even create proposals (my creative background helped), but I got little useful information on how to sell. The industry program that trains you to sell, Life Underwriters Training Course, was an option my general agent emphatically steered me away from. "You know more than they do. You don't need it," he said.

Instead, after I sold a few policies, he sent me to the Home Office Career School for five days, with this message: Mary is going to enroll in Chartered Life Underwriter (C.L.U.) classes and finish all ten courses in 2 years.

The Director of Training smiled and spent several hours during the week explaining patiently that earning a living with commissions and taking five C.L.U. courses each year were incompatible for a new recruit. I was grateful for his advice and returned to Miami with a scaled-down plan for ten courses spread over a five-year period, the typical agent pattern. That fall, in C.L.U., I found myself one of two women students. The other was an office manager and did no selling. It was the first time in my educational life I'd been the member of such a small minority. Casual friendships with the male students weren't easy to form, but I managed to make one friend and at the end of the first year I had passed C.L.U. 1 and earned $55,000 in commissions.

My new friend told me something I didn't know you could get and he didn't know I wasn't getting. It was called "financing."

This meant that for the first six months, year, or two or three, the insurance company underwrote trainees to help them earn while they learned. At that time, a typical financed new agent was "earning" $600 to $1,000 a month, guaranteed by the company. Of course, the salary was subtracted from earned commissions, but companies expected that the cost of training someone brand-new to insurance was the financing. My friend and I were both shocked when I blurted out that my company was not financing me and that this was the first time I had heard about it. In the first of a number of nonconfrontations, I did not take it up with my general agent, feeling that it was too late, that I'd been naive, and that I must pay the price.

Midway in the second year with this same general agent, my production and natural interests led me to be invited back for a second home office school, this time on business and estate planning. Recalling my original loneliness at being the only woman in a class, I tried unsuccessfully to have the company find another woman to enroll. "No one was qualified, no one was interested," they replied.

The class started off as might be expected: "Gentlemen, oh excuse me, and lady. . . ." Then the trainer recommended that we exchange room numbers so we could work on assignments between sessions. There was a dead silence. I gave my room number, there was another silence, then everyone (me included) laughed.

The thing which was so oppressive was that the whole situation was structured to teach men how to deal with men. I was a foreign element in a world with a completely different psychology. No one approached me at breaks; I felt very isolated.

That night I contemplated having dinner sent up to my room. But there was an attractive beer-and-shrimp bar downstairs, and I dressed up to go down there. In the bar, a classmate who watched me for half an hour came over and after a few drinks we had a very nice conversation: the first break in the ice. We were joined by three other men in the class. As they were all rather high, they decided they wanted to see Miss Nude Indiana perform in a local club. They were a little shocked when I invited myself along.

The next day, one of them informed me that I was okay, not like the woman who had attended his last class. She stayed in her room, hardly spoke and always had her nose in a book. I told him how tempted I had been to do the same thing. The training was not hard; dealing with the dynamics of male-female relations in a classroom setting was very difficult.

Nine months after that, I left the company. I was very angry about the lack of information about financing when I started, about the deliberate coldness of his other agents, and about my lack of sales training. I said nothing. I made an outside deal and withdrew.

I went to a company which asked me to develop a training program for women agents to form an all-woman unit. I was handed two women trainees—the wife of one agent and the mother-in-law of another. I found out later that my male peer selected his own trainees and took three or four months to do it, so as to be certain to get capable people.

There is a test administered to potential recruits to determine their suitability for insurance work. The basis for the decision was how much the applicant identified with successful men. There were also no materials to teach women how to sell to their natural clientele, other women. I tried to develop some.

We attended special training presented by a "top producer" with our students once a week. The trainer delighted in always calling on the less bright of my two students, and when she couldn't answer, saying to one of the men, "Tell her, Harry or Joe or. . . ." She dropped out of the class. One reason some of the men knew the answers, by the way, was because they were taking the course for the second time. All in all, the training was a fiasco, and I finally decided I couldn't invite women into that mess.

After this experience, I negotiated with a third company and became a general agent with my own office. I represent that company, but can sell policies of other companies which do not compete. Although I am permitted to recruit others, just as my first boss did, I do not nor do I expect to.

I have benefited a great deal from this experience: Now knowing much more about finance and business, my aspirations are higher, and my perspective on work and life is broader. It's quite an experience to learn what a human life is worth, and what the penalties for sickness, old age, and death are. Today, I'm more assertive and not as likely to be passive or withdraw from conflict, as I did over the financing business. I've proven that this stands me in good stead. As women are catapulted into the work world, they can't count on being taken care of by a husband or by the state.

I've also learned it's no fun being a "token." It's painful, and unless you can see you're just a step ahead of other qualified women who'll break down barriers by sheer numbers, it's seldom worth the personal cost of being the first one through the door.

5

Affirmative Action Offices: How They Can and Cannot Help

Dorothy D. Nevill
University of Florida
Gainesville, Florida

Little is known statistically about affirmative action officers employed by all types of institutions, but some insight can be gained concerning this office from an academic-settings study done by Gemmell.[1] Surveying 171 colleges and universities with enrollments of 10,000 or more, she found two types of affirmative action officers: full-time and part-time. The former position was usually held by a minority-group member and/or woman and carried a title such as affirmative-action or equal-employment officer. The latter was most often a white male and carried affirmative-action responsibilities in addition to other duties. Frequently, the title "affirmative-action officer" was merely tacked on to the position which the individual originally held, i.e., "personnel director and affirmative-action officer." In general, part-time officers

---

*Portions of this chapter were published in Dorothy D. Nevill, "Achieving Salary Equity," *Educational Record* 56(1975): 266-70.

were older and held more advanced degrees than did full-time officers. The median salary ranged from $15,000 to $19,999, with individuals earning more typically holding a doctorate and employed by larger institutions. Affirmative-action officers came from a wide variety of backgrounds, including psychology, counseling, sociology, law and business administration. However, regardless of the discipline from which they had come, the affirmative-action officers shared a common interest in working with people and in trying to understand the problems of women and minorities.

In describing a model affirmative-action plan which would be the most effective method of achieving equity for women and men, Weitzman[2] suggests that an affirmative-action officer be committed to the ideals of affirmative action and that all personnel involved in any aspect of the recruiting, hiring or promoting of employees be carefully screened and trained to insure that they set an exemplary model. Furthermore, she recommends that the affirmative-action officer work directly with the chief executive officer, have abilities and talents commensurate with that rank and be given an adequate staff to accomplish the task.

Unless an organization has a well-publicized affirmative-action policy, many women will be unaware that an affirmative-action officer even exists in her company or agency. Frequently, by scanning the "house newsletter" or by reading notices on bulletin boards, one can find the name, location and telephone number of the affirmative-action officer. If this fails, a glance at an organizational chart or inquiring among friends will usually root out the necessary information.

In general the affirmative-action officer is not in a direct administrative capacity, but functions as a staff assistant to a personnel officer, a vice president or some other line official. This very position in the organizational chart brings up one of the first issues that must be dealt with in understanding the role and function of the affirmative-action officer. This individual usually does not have direct authority to make changes in policy or procedure, but must work in conjunction with the officers of the company who can make this type of decision. Consequently, the affirmative-action officer falls into a no-one's land, caught between multiple constituencies: female employees, administrators, minority representatives, trustees or what-have-you.

What stance can the affirmative-action officer take and still survive? First of all, the position of "in-house revolutionary" is an untenable one. One cannot strongly attack those for whom one works and be an effective agent for change within that organization. Any call for radical change in an organization typically comes from outside that group.

The psychological climate which surrounds this position can be clearly seen in the responses to Gemmell's[3] questionnaire which revealed that affirmative-action officers view their situations as frustrating and lonely. The principal contributors to this feeling were seen as the inability to hold executives accountable for their actions, lack of budgetary authority and the staff nature of the job. However, lest we view the position of the affirmative-action officer in too negative a light, it should also be noted that these individuals reported a great deal of satisfaction in helping women and/or minority group members advance and prosper.

But what role can an in-house agent for change play? Basically the individual in this position has a choice between working within the establishment and of getting good press. If the specific task the affirmative-action officer must accomplish is to insure that women receive equal pay for equal work, that individual could assume either of two extreme stances. For example, one could use the office as a position from which to constantly and publicly exert pressure on the administration for higher salaries. However, if the affirmative-action officer chose to work within the system, she/he could work steadily in a low-keyed fashion for changes to be incorporated into the existing structure. The former stance earns one the love of one's constituency and publicity in the newspaper. Work within the system earns one the respect of other administrators and the feeling of being a team member. Some-how the affirmative-action officer must walk the tightrope between these two extremes, incorporating them both. The affirmative-action officer needs to gain the respect and confidence of both groups—management and employees.

It is therefore obvious that the affirmative-action officer is not a miracle worker who can alleviate a com-plaint with a nod of the head. But what then is the pur-pose of going to an affirmative-action officer? What can that person do?

Perhaps these types of questions can best be answered by looking at the major functions of that position. They can be divided into three main categories: handling infor-mal complaints, processing formal grievance procedures and overseeing affirmative-action programs.

Handling informal complaints occupies a major portion of the affirmative-action officer's time, yet goes relatively unnoticed except to the individuals involved. It is an important function because every case that can be resolved at this level is one which does not have to go on to the more formal grievance procedures.

A complaint usually begins with a telephone call to the affirmative-action officer. The matter can either be presented over the telephone or, preferably, an appoint-ment can be made so that face-to-face contact is possible. A woman should consider talking informally to the affir-mative-action officer for any type of complaint before going through more formal channels, if for no other reason than to gather information that might be helpful later. It could be that the affirmative-action officer can suggest alternative ways for a problem to be solved or can, through informal negotiations, resolve the difficulty.

It is here that the relationship between the affirma-tive-action officer and the line administrators of her/his organization is critical. If that individual is generally seen as strong yet cooperative, more will be accomplished than with a belligerent or antagonistic manner. It will work to a complainant's advantage if the affirmative-action officer is seen neither as a firebrand nor as a patsy, but as an independent team member. In all walks of life a large percentage of decisions are made on the basis of who is proposing the idea.

Through informal negotiations, a full spectrum of complaints can be resolved, from inadequate office space to unfair salary raises. Usually issues handled in this manner do not cause those involved to harden in their positions and be inclined to take the recriminative action that can accompany a more formal grievance procedure.

However, if the matter is not satisfactorily handled through informal negotiation, most organizations now have the option of a formal grievance procedure for all employees. Often there is a seperate procedure for cases related to sex/race discrimination. Usually the role of the affirmative-action officer is that of a mediator, an information gatherer and a recommender of specific action.

According to information released by the Equal Employment Opportunity Commission,[4] all grievance precedures should contain the following components:

1. There should be a standing (not *ad hoc*) grievance committee.
2. The committee should have relatively wide jurisdiction over all aspects of employment conditions.
3. Grievance procedures should allow for regular review.
4. Procedures should allow for a feedback mechanism in order to permit the institution to ascertain the employees' views about the procedures at regular intervals.
5. The grievance procedures should allow for top-level review of each situation.

An affirmative-action officer should be able to advise a woman of the proper procedures to follow if she wishes to press a more formal complaint.

Although procedures vary from organization to organization, it might be helpful at this point to describe one grievance procedure that is used by one institution. At the University of Florida a full-time affirmative-action coordinator works directly for the executive vice-president. In addition, there are part-time affirmative-action officers at each divisional level below the central administration. An employee who wishes to file a complaint does so with the appropriate lowest-level affirmative-action officer. Upon receiving the complaint, the officer investigates the case and makes certain that the complaint is brought to the appropriate head of the unit within which the alleged discriminatory acts occurred. If the complaint is not resolved at that level, then it is forwarded to successively higher levels until it reaches the office of the executive vice-president, who considers the complaint and either orders action to remedy the complaint or refers the matter to a grievance committee. If it is decided to have a grievance committee review the case, this committee is selected, partially by the employee and partially by the administration, from a pool of peers of the employees. A usually lengthy hearing then takes place, where both the employee and the administration present their case. Both present witnesses, evidence and testimony, and are represented by counsel. At the conclusion of any hearing, a written summary of the findings and recommendations arrived at by the grievance committee are forwarded to the president of the university who renders a final decision. At each step along the way the decision of whether to continue or not is at the discretion of the complaining employee.[5]

If a woman is considering a formal grievance, she should find out ahead of time from her affirmative-action officer what procedures should be followed.

The informal part of the affirmative-action officer's workload occupies a large amount of time, but not all informal activities are merely reflexive i.e., reacting to a complaint that has been presented. Equally important is the active searching out of possibly discriminating situations and rectifying them with positive steps. Informal negotiations by the affirmative-action officer can result in the hiring of a female vice-president, training courses for lower-echelon employees for possible advancement or a fair and equitable salary for all.

Such positive steps can also take place because of a definite commitment on the part of an institution or as a result of federal mandate. Whatever the source of impetus—the affirmative-action officer's energy, the goodwill of the administration or a nudge by a governmental agency—the affirmative-action programs undertaken by an institution are ones with which all employees should become familiar.

One of the most widely publicized affirmative-action programs has been that of achieving salary equity. That equal work deserves equal pay is a concept firmly established since the passage of the Equal Pay Act of 1963 prohibiting discrimination in salaries. Compensation to the victims of salary discrimination can be in the form of eliminating current salary differences between individuals who do comparable work or awarding back salary as a compensation for past inequities. Frequently both types of awards are made. Many of the settlements which have been made involve large sums of money or set landmark legal precedents. A brief synopsis of some of the most significant follows.

In May 1974, a new agreement between American Telephone and Telegraph (AT&T), the Equal Employment Opportunity Commission (EEOC) and the U.S. Departments of Labor and Justice was reached and resulted in the awarding of an estimated $30 million in back pay and salary adjustments to 25,000 female and/or minorities. AT&T, the nation's largest private employer, agreed to discontinue its practice of basing promotional increases on the employee's former salary and to establish minimum starting rates for all jobs within each salary group in the first two management levels.

Suits involving smaller amounts of money still benefit individuals. Continental Bank gave eight women employees back paychecks averaging $1,600 each plus salary increases as the result of an Equal Pay Act investigation by the U.S. Department of Labor. The women, who worked as assistant trust administrators, had been hired at job classification 8 and an average salary of $8,700. Men doing the same job had been assigned job classification 9 and a salary of $10,500. In another case, the U.S. Circuit Court ruled that Prince William Hospital Corporation of Manassas, Virginia, had violated the Equal Pay Act by paying female nurse aides less than male orderlies. Reversing a

district court decision, the Fourth Circuit Court of Appeals
stated that performing extra tasks such as heavy lifting
were not significant parts of orderlies' jobs. Two thousand
Western Electric Company employees shared an estimated
$800,000 in settlement of an EEOC complaint which
charged that before January 1970, the company had res-
tricted employees in its manufacturing divisions from
certain entry-level jobs and had delayed promotions. Two
Cleveland school teachers who took their suit against
mandatory maternity leave to the Supreme Court and won
a favorable judgment were granted back pay and court
expenses totaling more than $30,000 in U.S. District Court
on remand.[6]

Due to the above landmark decisions, organizations
have become increasingly interested in pursuing programs
to achieve salary equity. The choice lies between either
adopting a self-sponsored review of salaries or of facing
the possibility of doing so as a result of negotiations with a
federal agency or under court order. Usually institutions
relying on their own initiative (whether because of internal pressure from employees or because a spirit of fairness
permeates the organization) escape from having to award
back pay. However, those institutions which are not able
to demonstrate a past good-faith effort to adjust salaries
and make adjustments only as the result of a specific suit
are often punished by having to award back pay as well as
adjust current salaries. As an example of an active
approach to the role of an affirmative-action officer, two
approaches to correcting salary inequities are offered
below.

SALARY PREDICTION

There are various statistical procedures available for
an accurate assessment of salary structure. The classical
procedure is to compute averages for various categories
and compare these to each other. For example, a comparison could be made between the average salary paid to a
male bank teller and a female coworker. In a balanced
system where every category is represented by an equal
number of individuals, the classical method is perfectly

valid. But what if the numbers are not equal in each
category? What if the female bank tellers as a group have
significantly more experience than the male bank tellers?
In cases such as these, gross averages could be very biased
and misleading. Other variables could be having a weighty
influence. To better understand the problem let us work
through a common academic situation involving only two
variables, sex and degree.

	Ph.D.	M.A.
Male	Mean = $16,000	Mean = $12,000
	n = 200	n = 25
Female	Mean = $16,000	Mean = $12,000
	n = $10	n = 50

In this hypothetical situation, both females and males
receive an identical salary. However, when gross average
salary is computed, an apparent difference of nearly
$3,000 separates the sexes.

Male
$$\frac{200 \times \$16,000 + 25 \times \$12,000}{225} = \$15,555$$

Female
$$\frac{10 \times \$16,000 + 50 \times \$12,000}{60} = \$12,666$$

This apparent difference occurs because a high proportion
of the males have Ph.D. degrees, while a high proportion of
the females hold master's degrees. With equal numbers in
each category, we would obtain the same average for both
females and males ($14,000).

There are many other variables which can affect
salaries. The problem is to find a method which will
adequately juggle several influential factors at the same
time. There are several statistical methods available, the
most common of which is a multiple regression model.
This equation can be used to predict the expected salaries
of any individual employee with a given set of characteristics.[7]

Most of the work on multiple regression equations has
been done in academic settings. A wide range of variables
which contribute to the total salary has been identified,
including educational level, academic rank, administrative type, department, college, age, race, assignment, rank,

experience and so forth. A multiple regression equation is able to predict what would be the expected salary of an individual with any combination of the factors mentioned above. For example, the expected salary of an assistant professor in the English department with a doctorate and five years' experience could be determined; or that of a full professor in Engineering with a master's and twenty-five years' experience. Any discrepancy between the expected salary of the woman and the actual salary could be due to sex discrimination.

Several studies have clearly demonstrated a relationship between sex and salary. Gordon, Morton and Braden[8] in an investigation of the relationship between sex, race and discipline found that all three were significant variables. On the average a female faculty member earned 11 percent less than would be predicted for a man with her characteristics. Black faculty members earned 13 percent more than comparable whites. The effect of discipline is more difficult to summarize. In general a discipline is paid consistent with national demands. For example, a medical school faculty member with an M.D. was paid 93 percent more than a Ph.D. in the social sciences.

One of the major drawbacks to any statistical technique, including this one, is that measures which are difficult to quantify, such as special merit or ability, are often deleted from the equations. An investigation of average salary differentials at Southern Methodist University attempted to include more subjective measures[9]. The variables included were: (a) highest degree obtained, (b) ranking of the school from which the highest degree was obtained, (c) years in present faculty rank, (d) sex, (e) an index of university and professional service and of number of publications or artistic contributions, (f) level of faculty salary entrance rate for department and (g) the percentage of salary recovered from grants or contracts. The results indicated that approximately three-fourths of the female faculty members received salaries that were markedly below those of men with corresponding academic salaries and productivity, with individual differences ranging from 5 to 50 percent less. The authors concluded that the reasons for the discrepancies between salaries for men and women were probably due to an unconsciously narrow perception of women's roles and the peculiar relationship of many women to the external labor market.

In the largest study to date, Bayer and Astin[10] used data from the American Council on Education 1968-69 and 1972-73 surveys of college and university faculty members in a stepwise multiple regression model. They found that, although in the lower ranks salary differentials do not occur between men and women, the actual salary for female full professors was, on the average, $1680 lower than would be expected for male full professors who were statistically identical in terms of professional involvement, area of specialization, productivity, educational attainment and so forth.

Although any statistical method, including those mentioned above, has difficulty with variables which are hard to quantify, there are several advantages inherent in a statistical approach to achieve salary equity. Chief among these is that the onerous burden of pressing her own case does not fall on the individual woman. Instead, salary reviews are conducted as a matter of routine procedure.

COUNTERPARTING

Another method which is frequently used to adjust salaries is counterparting. The University of South Florida utilized this method as did the University of Florida. Although different locations can necessitate procedure modifications, the principles of counterparting remain essentially unchanged; i.e., the comparison of salaries of individuals of similar rank. At the University of South Florida, each department chairperson was asked to select a male counterpart for each female faculty member. Counterparts were selected on the basis of similar rank, experience and academic qualifications (including teaching, research and service) in the department. After the male counterpart was selected, the individual woman was asked whether or not she concurred. If she did, any salary discrepancy between the two faculty members was assumed to be the result of sex discrimination and appropriate salary increments were given. If the woman did not agree on the appropriateness of the selection made by the department chairperson, the matter was first referred to a departmental committee on faculty salaries, then to the dean of the college, and finally to the academic vice-president.[11] The method used at the University of Florida was similar except that the woman was able to select her own counterpart by negotiating with the department chairperson. In this instance, out of 75 women on the Education and General Budget who were considered eligible for counterparting, 58 shared in the awarding of some $65,000 in salary monies.[12]

There are several advantages inherent in this method of salary review. The method is a straightforward one which can be easily understood by all. Furthermore, although the individual woman is more heavily involved than in the salary prediction model and there is a greater chance of recrimination and ill-feeling, the procedure is still basically impersonal and does not require the female faculty member to initiate the proceedings.

In addition to plans for achieving salary equity, other affirmative-action commitments which any organization and affirmative-action coordinator can undertake are enumerated below.

1. Establishing training programs to prepare women and/or minority members for nontraditional fields.
2. Reviewing all hiring forms to ascertain that discriminatory language is not present (i.e., spouse's name instead of wife's name).
3. Setting up scholarship programs for educating potential future employees.
4. Monitoring hiring procedures to make certain that cultural stereotypes are not rigidly followed (i.e., all females, regardless of qualifications, are sent to interview for clerical positions).
5. Preparing presently employed female and/or minority group members for positions of higher responsibility.

6. Monitoring all aspects of working conditions to make certain that decisions are made on the basis of ability, not on shape or color of one's skin.

7. Developing company policy to make certain that a nondiscriminatory stance is shown in all aspects of the organization's internal and external relations.

8. Educating all employees about the principles of contract compliance and affirmative action.

9. Writing guidelines to be followed in the hiring, screening, selecting, interviewing, etc., of prospective employees.

10. Making certain that in a time of economic hardship the burden of termination does not fall more heavily on women and/or minorities and that any gain made by affirmative-action hiring is not obliterated.

11. Educating female and/or minority employees about their legal and ethical rights.

12. Screening all employment tests to make certain that they do not discriminate against any group or individual.

13. Taking positive steps to seek out and hire women and/or minority group members.

14. Developing plans for nondiscriminatory promotion schemes.

15. Creating an employment climate whereby each individual is judged solely on the basis of merit and ability.

The affirmative-action officer who even attempts to follow all of the suggestions outlined above will be a busy person indeed. Informal negotiations, formal grievance procedures and affirmative-action programs are all areas within which the affirmative-action officer should be knowledgeable and active.

6

A Case Herstory: Counterparting

Virginia E. Pendergrass
Florida International University
Miami

While I was busy writing this book, the Florida legislature was busy writing legislation. In 1976 the legislature passed a bill requiring each state university to determine whether women employees were discriminated against in salary as compared to male employees. If any inequities were found, the universities were ordered to correct the situations and report back to the legislature by the end of the year.

Our university chose to use the counterparting method to study women's and men's salaries. My program chair offered me the options of signing a waiver of claim (stating that I did not believe I was discriminated against on the basis of sex) or filling out a counterpart comparison and asking for a salary adjustment. I wouldn't have missed filing a claim for anything.

I was offered a number of resumes of men that my supervisors thought might be equivalent to me. After looking over several, I felt that I had better credentials than most hired at my rank. I inquired whether I was limited to choosing a person within my rank, and received a rather vague reply. So I deliberately chose a person who was hired at a higher salary *and* rank than I.

The legislation ordering the adjustment of women's salaries did not say anything about adjusting rank. The counterpart comparison that I prepared was as follows:

M E M O R A N D U M

TO: ———, Chairperson   DATE: July 8, 19—
FROM: Virginia E. Pendergrass,
Assistant Professor
SUBJECT: Salary Equity—Counterpart Study

This male counterpart has a degree which is equivalent to mine. He also holds a "terminal degree" in another field. I completed a postdoctoral traineeship in clinical psychology, which led to my licensure as a psychologist qualified to provide private clinical services in Florida. I was subsequently certified as a provider of psychological services by the National Council of Mental Health Providers.

This male had *5 years* postdoctoral experience prior to hiring at Florida International University. I had *3 years* of experience in private clinical and consulting practice, *1 year* of experience in research and *1 year* postdoctoral clinical study before employment at Florida International University. In addition, I had *4 years part-time* teaching experience at the college level, and had produced a number of publications in refereed national professional journals, presented at regional and national professional meetings. Finally, I had made substantial contributions at state, local and regional levels in voluntary and professional organizations boards and offices.

I believe that my qualifications at the time of

employment—my special experiences and attributes (professional and community service, record of research and publication) in addition to regular professional employment—were equivalent to the professional accomplishment of this male counterpart.

This male faculty member was hired to teach and advise students in an undergraduate program in 1973. I was hired in 1974 to perform the same academic services. He was hired at the rank of *associate professor* at a salary of $16,900; I was hired as an *assistant professor* at a salary of $15,500.

It has been my observation that when a male candidate is considered to be desirable, and his salary and/or rank demands exceed those purportedly available, adjustments are made to attract the male candidate. When I applied for employment, I requested the rank of associate professor and salary appropriate to the rank. These were refused. Since my qualifications equaled those of this male counterpart at the time of employment, I feel that I should also have been hired at the same rank and salary (associate professor/ $16,900).

My claim was approved by my chair and moved to the next level. After several days, I asked what had happened to the claim. The reply was complete double-talk, and I began to get a little suspicious. I asked for a written statement regarding the status of my claim. In reply I got a memo which stated that all counterparts selected by female faculty had been approved, but also stated that all claims had been referred to the "Salary Equity Committee."

I was surprised to discover that the claims had all been sent to the Salary Equity Committee, since we had understood that claims would be sent to this committee only if an administrator *disagreed* with our claim. Otherwise, we expected our claims to proceed directly up the line to the president for approval.

That was only the beginning of surprises. Many days

Florida International University
Counterpart Comparison(s) Format

	Person	Counterpart
Department/Office Unit	_____ FIU	_____ FIU
Names	Virginia E. Pendergrass	
Position Title	Assistant Professor	Associate Professor
Highest Degree	Ph.D.	Ph.D.
Area of Specialization	Experimental Psychology	Public Health Administration
Date Highest Degree	1969	1968
Other Training and/or Professional Development	Postdoctoral internship in clinical psychology (1 yr.) Specialist in school psychology Licensed by Florida Board of Examiners in psychology Noncredit workshops in NTL, gestalt, family therapy, women's issues, etc.	none shown
Professional Experience Since Degree	Clinical research associate (1 yr.) School psychologist (6 mos.) Private Practice (3 yrs.)	Regional Director—Health and Rehabilitative Services (1 yr.) Technical Assistance Officer—NIDA (2 yrs.) Program Coordinator to President for Development in Bahamas (1 yr.)

Other Professional Experience	Part-time teaching college level U of Miami (2 yrs.) MDCC (2 yrs.) U of No. Colorado (1 sem.) Barry College (1 sem.) Consultant in labor relations (1 yr.)	Assistant Regional Director—NIDA (3 yrs.) Public Health Officer (4 mos.) Community Development Advisor (1 yr.)

Counterpart Comparison(s) Format

Current Rank/Position	Assistant Professor	Associate Professor
Years in Rank/Position	2	2
Years at this University	2	3
Graduate of this University?	No	No
Publications/Papers/Presentations	12 professional publications 10 national/regional presentations 1 grant proposal (funded)	none shown
Honors and Awards	Two local civic Southeastern Psychological Assn. Visiting Woman Professor Board member and/or officer in regional and local professional organizations (3)	none shown
Special Attributes/Experience		National professional association memberships (2)

This counterpart analysis was revised to protect the identity of the male counterpart; job titles are similar to those of the male counterpart but not exactly those shown in resume.

41

later, several women told me they had been called into a meeting with a male faculty member who represented the Salary Equity Committee. He was also a lawyer, which the women felt was somewhat intimidating. Each woman was told that the committee had found no evidence of sex discrimination, and the lawyer refused to discuss any reasons for the decisions. Each woman was asked to sign statements accepting the finding or asking for appeal. I returned the two statements asking for an appeal, and included a cover memo asking for the basis for this decision.

I never heard from the Salary Equity Committee again.

Not one single claim in our whole division was allowed by the Salary Equity Committee, which soon became known as the Salary Inequity Committee. In a stroke of genius, the administration had appointed the following members to the committee: 1) a female vice-president of the university, 2) a (female) director of the Office of Minority and Women's Affairs and 3) a male faculty member (lawyer). Furthermore, both women on the Salary Equity Committee asked for and received substantial salary adjustments very early. I expect that I don't need to expand upon the feelings that this situation engendered.

Finally, we women began to get together, and I found that others had fared even worse than I. Some said they were threatened ("there are plenty of women out there who would be glad to work for your salary"); some were ordered to accept counterparts they felt were unsuitable. Some were refused access to information regarding salaries and backgrounds of potential counterparts.

To cap it all off, a number of our male colleagues were outright hostile. Some felt "unqualified" women were using the legislation to unjust purpose. Some apparently felt that the comparisons would embarrass them, since they were very angry if it became known that they had been chosen as counterparts. The rumor began to run around that men would not receive merit raises because women were getting all the "raise" money in salary adjustments.

When we women got together, it became clear that the administration of the university was trying to quash nearly all of the claims. Interestingly, if *every single claim* had been fully granted, it probably would have required less money than that appropriated by the legislature for our university.

Other women reported that they had examined their files and found critical memos of which they had not been informed and to which they had had no chance to respond. I trotted off to see my file, and sure enough, I found such a memo, to which I immediately responded:

M E M O R A N D U M

TO: Dr. _____ , Salary Equity Commission
                 DATE: July 13, 1976
FROM: _____ , Assistant Dean
SUBJECT: COUNTERPART STUDY — RE:
                 DR. VIRGINIA PENDERGRASS

Several problems have been raised by Dr. Pendergrass to support alleged sex discrimination in salary. The counterpart and Dr. Pendergrass have had comparable experiences, although Dr. _____'s experiences were national rather than locally oriented. The major complaint seems to be related to the rank awarded during hiring. For the rank of Associate Professor, the mean salary in faculty lines at that time in the School (1973-1974) was approximately $16,000 as compared to a $12,000-$15,900 range for the Assistant Professor. The refusal of the Program to afford an Associate Professorship seems more related to salary dollars available in a line rather than sex in the counterpart's gender identity.

Recommendation:
A more complete analysis of this challenge should be made by the Ad Hoc Salary Equity Committee using

more specific criteria. Thus, a dollar differential cannot be made.

(INTER-OFFICE COMMUNICATION)
****

M E M O R A N D U M

TO: _____, Vice-President for   DATE: 9/5/—
               Academic Affairs
FROM: Virginia E. Pendergrass, Social Work Pro-
               gram
SUBJECT: Salary Equity Study

In examining my file on Salary Equity in the Dean's office, I discovered that a memo from ——— has been included in materials sent to the Salary Equity Committee which had not been discussed with me. I was surprised to find this memo in the file since I had specifically asked———to communicate to me her analysis of my materials after she had examined them. In response to this verbal request, she did indeed distribute a memo, but the memo did *not* include very significant information sent in her memo to the Salary Equity Committee.

I am concerned about the progress of the Salary Equity Study, especially in regard to my own situation. Some of my concerns are:

1. It was my understanding that no materials would be submitted to the Salary Equity Committee unless there was a dispute between the complainant and the chair, the dean or the vice-president. My chair, ———, concurred in my choice of counterpart and my request for remediation. ——— (the dean's designee in his basence) did *not* discuss any dispute with me before submitting the materials to the Salary Equity Committee.

2. I feel that if ——— had reservations which warranted the materials being submitted to the Salary Equity Committee, she should have discussed them with me first, and I should have been acquainted with the memo she was submitting which subsequently appeared in my file.

3. I do not feel that the remarks ——— made in the memo are useful or relevant in evaluating my complaint, on the following basis:

   a. while ——— points out that my male counterpart had "national" experience as opposed to my extensive involvement in community organizations, professional associations and in scholarly activities leading to substantial publications, which the *male* did not have;
   publications, which the *male* did not have;

   b. I am indeed contending that the rank awarded me was less than I deserved, and I pointed out in my memo that in my experience in the university system, there is quite a bit of flexibility in terms of adjusting rank and salary to meet the needs of "attractive" candidates. ———'s memo implies that indeed the rank and salary were there in my case.

   To claim that the action was not discriminatory because it occurred at the "program" level and not in the dean's office is ridiculous. This action was approved by authorized agents of the university, including the chair, the dean, the vice-president for academic affairs and the president, as are all faculty appointments. In hiring, the faculty's perception of "quality" in a candidate is just as affected by the pervasive prejudice against female candidates as are perceptions elsewhere. It is the responsibility of the administration of the university to ensure that equal opportunity in employment is afforded to all. I do not believe this was done in my case.

   I feel that it was highly improper for documents to be submitted along with my complaint without my knowledge, for deliberations to be held in secret with no opportunities to respond to negative information, and I again question the entire procedure, as well as the decision communicated to me by the Salary Equity Committee. I do not feel that I had any opportunity for a full and fair hearing in this matter.

I am requesting that after your review of these materials, you direct the following actions be taken:
1. adjust my salary, as of date of employment, to $16,900;
2. adjust my rank, as of date of employment, to Associate Professor

in compliance with the intent of HB1104 and other existing equal employment legislation.

In order to try to head off final negative decisions by the president which would necessitate legal suit, we tried to get an appointment with the president—without success. Finally, one women maneuvered her way onto the agenda of a hearing of the state education board and publicly raised the question of the salary equity study at our university. Interestingly, she was invited to a meeting with the president the same day. After a few skirmishes, the vice-president began to meet with each woman individually regarding her claim. Many of the women received offers that they felt were acceptable, and signed documents to that effect. I did not fare so well, as shown in the following summary by the vice-president:

MEMORANDUM

TO: President   DATE: October 21, 1976
FROM: Vice-President
SUBJECT: COUNTERPART SALARY CLAIM FOR
             VIRGINIA E. PENDERGRASS

I met with Dr. Pendergrass regarding her salary equity, but have not arrived at an agreement. I have proposed that her salary be increased $499, $500 less than the counterpart she had chosen. The reason for the differential is that while she is an assistant professor, he is an associate professor. The salaries currently are $15,500 and $16,499, respectively. The counterpart also has had his Ph.D. one year longer and been on the FIU faculty one year longer than Dr. Pendergrass. I pointed out to Dr. Pendergrass that if and when she is promoted to associate professor she would receive an automatic $500 promotional increase, making their salaries the same.

Part of the problem is that Dr. Pendergrass feels that she deserves retroactive pay adjustments and she should have been promoted earlier to associate professor. This part of her claim I refuse to deal with.

I call to your attention the fact that the Salary Equity Committee recommended no salary change.

Since I was unable to reach accord with Dr. Pendergrass I have asked her to make an appointment with you to review her claim.

cc: Assistant Vice-President

****

After meeting with the vice-president, I immediately asked to see the president. In the meeting with the president (and vice-president) I could get nowhere on the rank issue. The administration's argument was that the legislation which enabled the salary adjustments said nothing about rank. The vice-president admitted that he had made a mistake in computing my counterpart's salary and raised his offer from $500 to $1,000. I agreed to accept $1,000.

At this point, our women's group more or less disbanded, since it appeared that satisfactory settlements were being reached.

Hah!

Many of the women who had signed statements of agreement with the vice-president were notified that the president "did not accept the vice-president's recommendation," and that the president was reducing the amount agreed upon. In some cases,the offer was withdrawn

altogether. Most of these women are now being represented by the union to insure that the university lives up to
the agreements negotiated by the vice-president. There are
also still a few women who were never able to reach a settlement (the "troublemakers"?).

My offer was not withdrawn. I can only surmise that
this is because I reached my agreement with the vice-
president in the president's office, while the others reached
agreement privately with the vice-president.

The last straw was the basis for awarding "merit"
increases, which took place soon after. In our school, every
person whose salary was "below the average for his/her
rank" was awarded an increase. Is it possible that those
whose "salaries were below average for their ranks" were
men, and women who had waived a claim in the salary
equity study ("good" women)?

All in all, the counterparting effort was a mess. At the
very least, however, we have a lot of women whose simple
faith in the benevolence of administrators is seriously
shaken, and who may be better prepared in the future to
recognize and deal with discriminatory practices. We
learned a lot about our adversaries and our resources.

7

The Local
Civil Rights Agency

Claire F. Mitchel
Broward County Human Relations Division
Fort Lauderdale, Florida

In a recent interview, Gloria Steinem was asked to comment on the death of the women's movement. She responded, "The women's movement is pronounced dead at least once a week. But movements go through stages, some overt and some less overt. At the beginning women were in the streets demonstrating. Then the movement went through a diagnostic stage, studying institutions that needed to be changed. Now we're at an uncomfortable place where women have a lot of expectations and a lot of popular support with institutions that are changing too slowly. It is a time of maximum tension between raised expectations and a reality that won't budge." The same is true of other civil rights movements.[1,2]

To bridge this difficult time in Florida, the Broward County Human Relations Division (HRD) was formed. The HRD is charged with the "protection of human rights." Within HRD, the Women's Concerns section ". . . acts as

49

women's advocate . . . for elimination of discriminatory
practices in employment, housing, public accommoda-
tions, and educational opportunities within Broward
School System, serves on the Title IX Committee and as a
general support for improving the conditions of wom-
en. . . . "[3,4] In the area of employment we send staff to
speak publicly against discrimination and for affirmative
action; we refer complaints to other agencies; we invite
and investigate individual complaints, and we assist busi-
nesses in implementing affirmative-action programs. The
agency has no enforcement powers and acts as advisor and
conciliator only.[5]

EMPLOYMENT DISCRIMINATION COMPLAINTS

Inviting the complaint. "If you feel you have been
discriminated against when you look for a job or housing,
Broward County's Human Relations Division may be able
to help you," the ad states. Such ads appear in newspaper
employment columns, radio, and TV public service
announcements.

Applications for assistance from HRD increased from
eleven to thirty-three a month within thirty days of the
start of the TV public service announcements. Staff also
speak on radio and TV, before clubs and agencies and in
newspaper interviews.

We also distribute a red-white-and-blue folder entitled *Defending Your Job Rights:*

DISCRIMINATION IS UNLAWFUL in employment because of race,
color, religion, sex or national origin and is prohibited by TITLE VII
of the Civil Rights Act of 1964.

The law also prohibits your employer, employment agency or labor
organization to punish you because you have filed charges or spoken
out against any employment practice made unlawful by Title VII.

You have a right to complain if: an employer refuses to hire you
when you are qualified for a job opening; refuses to let you file an
application but accepts others; you are passed over for a promotion
for which you are qualified; you are paid less than others for comparable work; a union or employment agency refuses to refer you to a

job opening or refuses to accept you into membership because of your race, color, national origin, religion or sex.

The Equal Employment Opportunity Act of 1972 provides for a woman to be treated no differently from a man when she seeks, holds or leaves a job.

The law covers private and public employers of fifteen or more employees, employment agencies, labor organizations, training programs, and the federal government under special conditions. Only when a charge is filed by a person will the HRD or any governmental agency take action.

In 1976, more than 150 employment discrimination complaints were filed with Broward County HRD, of which 31 charged sex discrimination. Of these, 24 were pursued and 16 were either resolved, withdrawn or pending. Eight were sent on to the Equal Employment Opportunity Commission regional office in Miami for processing under the Civil Rights Act of 1964.

Women who have filed with EEOC have usually been employed in schools and management echelons of private industry.[6] Now, fortunately, the HRD is reaching women of middle and lower occupational and educational status: saleswomen, food inspectors, bartenders, technicians, among others.

Documenting the complaint. The majority of employment discrimination complaints filed with HRD are initiated by telephone. The complainant is usually angry and vents this on the first person who will listen—the phone receptionist. Her/his empathetic response can be a deciding factor in whether or not the aggrieved person enters and successfully completes a complaint.

During the first call, the phone receptionist will fill out an inquiry information sheet to determine whether the complaint comes under HRD jurisdiction; i.e., discrimination due to race, color, religious creed, sex or national origin. Although the law does not cover the handicapped, we also process complaints of discrimination in this area.

If the complaint does not come under HRD purview,

we attempt to refer it to the proper agency. If we can act, we set up a file to keep track of all correspondence, phone calls and meetings. An appointment is made with a staff member.

When the complainant arrives, the staff member will try to cover the following points: How were other people treated differently? Has a complaint been filed with a state or federal agency? With the company, union, etc.? Has a complaint of this nature ever been filed before? What reasons were given for rejection, being fired, etc.? The complainant will be asked for names and addresses of those who can back up her story.

The worker then writes a narrative report of the event, which is immediately typed. An EEOC-5 form (January 1972) Charge of Discrimination is filled out, signed by the complainant and notarized. If the person does not wish to be identified, HRD may file a "third person" complaint without using her name.

Investigating the complaint. The investigator will then telephone the employer to ask for an interview. The employer will be assured that the investigator is interested in the *facts.*

The investigator will first request to review the complainant's personnel record. She/he will be alert to any discrepancies between the complainant's account and the documentation in the personnel file. The investigator will especially note absenteeism, evaluations, memos regarding performance, promotions/demotions, pay changes and other information. The investigator will also look for possible witnesses and record comments made by the employer and witnesses. Payroll stubs, application forms or other documents may be gathered. Many instances of bias are so subtle that even the·victim may not recognize some information which is valuable to the case.

After the conference with the employer, which the investigator attempts to conclude on a cordial note, she/he will review the information.

If the complaint does not appear well founded, the investigator meets with the complainant to explain why. Even so, the complainant is never discouraged from proceeding with the EEOC.

The investigator, however, need only find reasonable cause to believe that discrimination occurred; it does not have to be established beyond a shadow of a doubt. If there does appear to be discrimination, the investigator will arrange a meeting with both the respondent and the complainant present. The employer who is reluctant to meet is informed that discrimination is against the law, and that while everyone would like to handle the matter on a local level, the charging party can file with the EEOC. Many employers will agree there has been a violation when confronted with well-organized evidence. The complainant may then request whatever settlement she wishes, and the negotiations begin. When the claimant and respondent are able to agree upon a settlement, they will sign a document giving the details of the settlement and stating the claimant's willingness to drop charges without a lawsuit.

Unfortunately, if no agreement can be reached, the EEOC will be slow to act. The EEOC, the only federal enforcement agency which deals exclusively with discrimination, had a backlog of over 100,000 complaints in 1976.[7]

Cases in Point. A pregnant X-ray technician was asked to leave her job because she was "incapacitated"; she filed charges of sex discrimination with the HRD. The hospital agreed to take back the woman, with back pay and with maternity leave, after she brought a note from her gynecologist saying her present pregnancy would not be affected by the work any more than her first child had been under similar conditions.

Another woman who was earning $6,000 a year applied for an upgrading of her position in her firm. Her qualifications were appropriate, but when she was interviewed for the request, she felt the interviewer was hostile. Her request was denied. She filed with HRD and the HRD investigator negotiated to have her re-interviewed by someone outside the personnel department. She is now in the higher-ranking job earning over $9,000 a year.

Keeping sales records enabled an appliance saleswoman to prove that, given equal chances on the floor of a large chain store, she sold more than male coworkers. HRD argued against her transfer to a salaried, lower-paying department and the company decided in the employee's favor. By the time of conciliation, the woman had moved out of town and did not want to return to that job.

AFFIRMATIVE ACTION

The HRD also assumes the role of helping public and private organizations develop affirmative-action plans. *A Guide to Affirmative Action in Employment* (Broward County Community Relations Commission, 1974) gives employees step-by-step information necessary to fulfill a commitment to erase any underutilization of minorities and women in a work force, and to establish goals and timetables.[8,9]

To find out if an employer is in compliance, there are some basic questions: Are most women in lower-paying jobs? Do pay scales differ for men and women? Are lines of promotion closed to women? Do men and women receive the same fringe benefits for their spouses and dependents?

On occasion, the HRD may also be asked to determine whether a prospective government contractor can be expected to comply with equal opportunity legislation. The county can thus be advised whether a contractor is eligible for public funds.

8

A Case Herstory: Negotiating a Settlement

Anonymous

I graduated with a degree in interior design and marketing and looked for my first job in Dade County, Florida. I applied at a local design studio in a major furniture corporation, hoping to get into their design studio as an assistant. There was nothing open except in their computer room. I took this job to get my foot in the door.

After only three weeks, the store manager offered me an assistant's position where I could learn buying and merchandising. I took it, thinking I would move over to design after I learned buying and merchandising.

I married a coworker a few months later, and had to move to another location, since the corporation did not allow spouses to work in the same store. Next my husband was transferred to Atlanta and I went with him. We separated soon after that and I returned to Dade County.

I heard of a new opening in the design studio and

asked to interview for it. When I arrived for the interview, the studio director suggested we go to a more "comfortable" location, which turned out to be a private club. He suggested that if I went to bed with him, he would hire me. I was very insulted and dropped the application.

A position in carpet sales came open in this same furniture chain in Broward County (a few miles north). I took it. I was the first saleswoman in the department. I was told that it would take about six months for me to learn the business and level off in terms of my sales, but then it would be a very well-paying job. A person in carpet sales makes a minimum of $12,000 a year. My first day on the job I sold $5700 worth of carpet, and every day after I was the top seller. After only a few weeks, the "best" store (the main one in Dade County) asked that I be transferred to them.

When I got there, things did not go well. Usually the store manager (who is salaried) will work with a new employee to help at the beginning, and all commissions will go to the new employee. After a few weeks, the store manager will shift to another employee or will work with the weakest salesperson to help get their production up. When I arrived, I asked the store manager for help, but he refused. I found out that he did not work with anyone, but assigned all his sales to *one* man in the department, even when we were all present and sales should have been divided evenly. Still, without help, I was never the worst salesperson and usually came in right behind the store manager's pet in sales.

I was also the *only* woman salesperson in this store; I was told that the women in office and secretarial positions were mad at me because they were not allowed to move from the office to sales, which paid up to $30,000 a year. This annoyed me because I wasn't just somebody off the street. I had worked in every branch of that business and had a good sales record at the first store, which was why I was transferred to this job.

After about ten days, the district manager told me my sales were "falling behind." I told him that I had only been there ten days and that my sales record was as good as anyone else's even though I was new.

The next day was my day off. The district manager called me at home and told me I was fired. He "wanted someone stronger." I found out later that a friend of his needed a job, and he got rid of me to make an opening.

I was very upset. I had never been fired before. I called the Broward County store and asked if I could come back. They said they'd be delighted. That was very reassuring. The next day, however, they said no. Obviously they had gotten the word from the main store.

I knew that if an employee is on probation (sixty days), she can be fired without recourse. After that, however, the employee is entitled to three corrective interviews, and a reason must be given for dismissal. I had been fired on the sixty-first day of my employment, and of course no interviews were given. I went to the personnel coordinator for the whole corporation and complained. He thought it was funny. I told him I would go to women's groups or sue or do whatever was necessary to get this taken seriously.

After he "investigated," he called me back and said I was fired because I couldn't do floor plans, which was ludicrous, because I was the only person in that department trained in interior design. He called back a second time and said I was fired because I wouldn't move floor samples. I told him that I was hired as a salesperson, not a warehousewoman, and asked him to show me a job description which included moving carpets around.

He then said I was fired because my shipping averages were low—you will notice that he did not mention "sales." The difference is that sales are transactions on the floor, which then have to be made into orders, sent to the central warehouse, and finally the order will be shipped. So it takes about three weeks for sales to appear in shipping records. Since I had been at the store only ten days, I could hardly have high shipping averages. But I did have sales, and I had all the paperwork and deposits and everything else required, so my shipping orders would have been high three weeks later!

When I heard this, I asked for a copy of the daily sales records from the corporation's lawyer. The daily sales records listed each employee and the dollar amount of

sales for each. The personnel coordinators had blanked out
the amount of sales for everyone but me, so that I couldn't
compare my sales with the others. I made the lawyer
initial these copies, so that he couldn't claim later that I
had changed them. Then I got copies of the originals. My
sales, in black and white, were as good as, or better than,
everyone except the store manager's pet.

I went to the Broward County Human Relations Division and also filed a claim with the fair housing and
employment agency in Dade County. I did not hear anything from the fair housing office, but the Broward County
HRD called immediately. They contacted the store and the
store offered to settle. I think the other women in the store
were getting antsy and the store hoped to get everything
calmed down. The first thing the store did was to offer me
a job as a secretary at $110 a week. I was really broke and
took it. I did not withdraw my complaint like they thought
I would.

I was transferred out of the store to a central warehouse, where I did not have to be in contact with the same
people. I got a really great boss and loved the work I was
doing. Since there were only three of us on the location,
everyone did everything. I made out orders, dealt with
customers, everything.

Then the corporation offered to give me $2000 if I
would drop my complaint and resign within thirty days, or
if I dropped the charges and didn't ask for money, I could
keep the job I now had. We argued back and forth and the
offer got up to $2500 and I could keep the job as long as I
performed satisfactorily. Finally, the personnel coordinator told me that my boss had said he was "not satisfied"
with my performance.

I was really hurt, because I liked my boss and he had
always said I was doing an outstanding job. I was afraid
the company was building up another case to fire me, and I
went to my boss to ask him if he had said that. He said that
he did not say it, but if the corporation told him he said it,
he would agree in public.

When I was fired before, I was so broke that my
telephone was disconnected. I didn't have anything in the
bank. My salary was now only about $90 a week; I had to

work two and one half weeks of the month just to pay my mortgage. I finally agreed to sign.

I arrived to sign the release and the personnel coordinator, the corporation's attorney and the state's attorney were all there. Everyone was chipper, except me. I told them I would only sign under these conditions:

1) that within a reasonable period of time, my salary was raised to a reasonable level; and

2) that if any other act of discrimination occurred, I would renew my claim.

They told me there was no time to retype the agreement, but that the corporation would agree to those requirements. I asked all eight persons to witness that the corporation agreed.

I signed the agreement in October. I worked fifty to sixty hours a week from October to December because I really liked my job, but I still got the same low salary. Finally, my boss said I was doing so well, he would give me a raise of $10 a week. A month later, he asked if the raise had come through. I told him no, and he gave me $40 cash. Three months later, still no raise in my paycheck.

Also, a minor thing which irks me: When the corporation had its annual Christmas party, everyone was invited except me. Another employee called me to ask if I was going and I told him I hadn't been invited. He called the office to "ask if I could come"—mind you, I was an employee and every other employee was invited. They grudgingly "gave permission."

Six months later, the fair housing agency in Dade County discovered my claim on their desk. They called to find out whether I still wanted to pursue the claim. I was really fed up with my low salary, no raise, being ignored. I told them the whole story, and they said the agreement I signed was not valid since the job was in Dade County and the agreement was negotiated in Broward County.

When the corporation got wind of this, they asked me to sign new papers. They assumed I would sign. About this time, a raise of $8 a week finally turned up in my paycheck.

I told them I felt they had not lived up to their agreement to give me a reasonable salary in a reasonable

time. Men in the company doing my job were making twice
as much as I was. They said I was "just a secretary" and
made the salary I deserved. Meanwhile I did all the merchandising, a job comparable to assistant buyer, executive
secretary and merchandiser.

The interviewer at the fair housing agency advised me
to re-open the case. What I would like is a salary equivalent to what I would have been making if I had stayed in
the sales position; I'm not even making half that now. I
expect, though, that the corporation will give me a cash
settlement and make me leave the company. They say they
will give me good recommendations if I decide to go. It's
funny that they think I'm so good but they won't give me a
decent job themselves, knowing that I am and always have
been a loyal and hard-working employee.

I have tried to remain friendly and ladylike, but it is
very difficult to deal with them like that. They get so
enraged at my challenging what they are doing. It has been
very hard to live like this with no money. I'm used to
having nice things in my home and wearing nice clothes,
but now I just barely pay for the essentials and stay home.
I have to work like a dog and make the same salary as the
company's maid.

9

Academic Women and Unions

Joyce Peterson
Florida International University
Miami

A popular song of the CIO organizing drive of the 1930s told of the union maid who would "always organize the guys" and advised other women to marry union men and join the ladies' auxiliary.

Times have changed. Women in universities today, influenced by the two streams of the women's liberation movement and a movement for faculty power embodied in unions, are out to organize themselves, along with their male colleagues, into collective bargaining organizations. They expect these unions to meet the special needs of often discriminated-against women as well as the needs of all faculty members.

Traditionally universities have been bastions of the individual approach to making a way in the world. The individual professor was hired through his or her professional contacts (the old *boy* network), bargained for a salary in the dark about what colleagues received, and moved up or off the academic ladder according to his/her ability to meet often unspecified criteria of publication and congeniality.[1] The system is changing, particularly in the large public universities where faculty are beginning to organize into unions and bargain collectively for a contract which governs their professional life. The growing tendency for university professors to embrace unions coincides with the increasng awareness of women academics that sex discrimination is real and can be fought. The two trends have much in common and each can derive strength from the other. One of the most effective ways for women to fight against discriminatory hiring, salary, promotion, and tenure policies is by seeing that their needs are met in union contracts that they help write and negotiate.

On many campuses, teacher unionism is a relatively new phenomenon. This means that women have an especially good opportunity to make their voices heard since they will not have to fight against entrenched union opposition to women sharing power with men. In addition, young unions usually need all the active members they can find and positions of leadership are frequently available to women willing to do the work.

How Unions Can Help Women

In the same way that unions help any workers by providing them with the strength of collective action as opposed to the weakness of solitary battles, unions can help women. In practice, this means many things. To many women, one of the most important benefits of unionization will be the union contract.[2] This contract should include a clause binding both the university and the union to a policy of nondiscrimination. In addition, a contract will usually include a clear statement of the promotion process and a salary scale which automatically eliminates some sources of salary inequality. In general, the earnings gap between men and women is less for union members than for nonmembers.[3]

One of the problems that women have traditionally faced in trying to enforce antidiscrimination policies is acquiring the information necessary to make a case. Union contracts can require that the university regularly provide the union with complete information on the title, salary, and tenure status of all members of the bargaining unit.

This can be particularly helpful in grievance cases which arise out of instances of discrimination against women. The contract will provide for a reasonably rapid-moving procedure which allows the union to represent aggrieved members before the administration. Anything in the contract has the effect of binding law and can be the subject of a grievance procedure if not adhered to. It is, therefore, particularly important to women that their special needs be met and included in the contract.

Besides issues of hiring, promotion, salary, and tenure, women may use a union contract to assure themselves of nondiscriminatory fringe benefits. Medical insurance should include abortion and maternity coverage available to both single and married women. In addition, retirement plans should not discriminate against women for living longer than men.[4]

A union-negotiated contract may also provide for leaves of absence for childbearing with the right to return to one's former position. Such leaves may also be available to all parents, men or women, who desire leave to care for newborn infants.

Since women faculty members are often heavily represented in the part-time classification, they frequently find themselves without fringe benefits or any possibility of job security. Union contracts have been successful in granting commensurate fringe benefits for part-time faculty and in instituting tenure ladders which accommodate part-time teachers.

One of the most powerful concepts used by women and minorities in recent years to help redress past discriminatory practices on the part of colleges and universities is affirmative action.[5] Many colleges now have some sort of affirmative-action program drawn up by administrators. In some cases, affirmative-action programs have become part of union contracts. This can be extremely important for women who desire to pursue a case against the university based on its failure to comply with an affirmative-action program. If a faculty member wants to challenge the university on a violation of its affirmative-action program or any other matter covered in the contract, she is able to do so with the weight of the union behind her. This is much different than one lone woman, with perhaps a few friends backing her, taking her case through the long, complicated, often mystifying, and increasingly hostile process of grievance pressing. In very concrete terms, union support may mean such things as legal advice and union representatives to negotiate for her. In more general terms, the knowledge of union support may mean a great deal in maintaining morale through an extremely trying experience. When other people agree that her rights have been violated and must be restored (and have the weight of legal agreement behind them), it is easier to continue to believe that her case is just and winning is possible.

How Unions May not Help

In the past, unions have often shown little interest in women members and have contributed to male supremicist leadership.[6,7] There are still problems, and none of the previously mentioned benefits are likely to be automatically awarded as prizes to women for signing a membership card.

Union men, brothers though they be, have been subjected to the same sexist upbringing as everyone else and may often be insensitive, if not hostile, to the needs of their female colleagues. In addition, white male professors seem frightened by any signs of increasing numbers of black and women faculty and are prone to such comments as "Pretty soon there won't be any faculty members who aren't black or women." They can also have wildly unfactual ideas about how much money women make—ideas that can be effectively punctured by a simple display of the facts showing how women's salaries stack up against men's at each rank.

Women within unions have a double job on their hands. One is to assure that women union members receive equitable treatment from the university. This is why women faculty members join unions; they also join because men and women faculty members have many common problems and needs and it makes sense to join collectively in establishing themselves as a powerful bargaining force.

The second job facing women in unions is to see that they receive equitable treatment from the union and that women's demands become union demands. In dealing both with the problems of presenting the needs of women to the university and articulating women's special concerns, and in struggling against sexism within the union, a women's rights committee is very helpful. Many faculty unions already include women's rights committees in their organizational structure. In other cases, it may be necessary for women to form such a committee and demand that it be recognized as part of the union's structure. Such a committee can serve a variety of ends. It can have primary responsibility for developing union programs that particularly affect women. Contract issues centering on affirmative action, protection against discriminatory hiring, salary, promotion or tenure practices, day-care facilities, and child-bearing and child-care leaves might be the special responsibility of the women's rights committee. These issues must all become the concern of the union as a whole and should not be considered as of interest to women alone, but initially they are likely to be stated most correctly if women work them out. The women's rights committee might also work to collect information about women in the university and to publicize their needs.

Some of the more subtle problems of women in mixed female-male organizations can also be brought to light in a women's rights committee. Men need to be made aware when they fail to listen if a woman is speaking, when they crack jokes at the expense of women, when they make assumptions about ability that lead to comments like "I wouldn't want to hire a woman just because she's a woman."

All in all, union membership offers women academics an excellent chance to defend and promote their interests within the university while at the same time building a genuine coalition with men who share their problems as faculty members. There are benefits that extend beyond the university as well, for the local union's ties to other locals and to national leadership afford the possibility of influencing labor's attitude to questions of women's rights. They also provide lobbying pressure upon state and national legislatures to push for legislation of interest to women, including the Equal Rights Amendment.

Finally, union membership provides a common bridge to other union women. Professional women, active in feminist causes, have often lamented their inability to interest working-class women. The commonality of union membership provides a place to begin a dialogue about the needs of women workers which could be very exciting and fruitful.

10

A Case Herstory: A College Women's Committee in Action

Anonymous

Editor's Note: The following case herstory illustrates representation of a woman by an informal group (a college women's committee), with the understanding that the union will intervene if the administration does not respond to informal pressure. While unions bring their full power to bear when they file formal grievances and legally represent the union member, unions also frequently attempt to negotiate satisfactory settlements before filing formal complaints. An effective union representative would use many of the same tactics in documenting performance and conferring with administrators.

In spring 1972, I was hired at A College, a unit of B University, to replace a woman who would retire in the fall. She had interviewed me and strongly endorsed my qualifications to teach her courses. During the summer, before my appointment was to begin, I became seriously ill. My new chairman readily granted me a leave of absence for the fall semester. I learned later that his department was overstaffed; after hiring me, he created another opening for a less qualified man with political influence. This is an example of the buddy system in action.

I planned to arrive before the start of the spring semester to prepare a new course. Medical complications, however, prevented my early arrival, and I informed the chairman that I would be delayed. I did so using a casual postcard, which he regarded as "flippant." His reply stated that he objected to the tone of my postcard, that he had been personally inconvenienced by having to order my teaching materials for me, and that "non-reappointment" decisions for the following year would have to be made soon after my arrival.

As an experienced academic person, I understood the implications of his language. He had already decided on a "non-reappointment," rather than a reappointment. I arrived for the spring semester with a clean bill of health and an expectation of trouble; I therefore lost no time in joining the union, and the College Women's Committee (CWC), which is the local campus chapter of the University Women's Committee.

From the outset, the chairman indicated that the "non-reappointment" classroom observation would take place very soon. It occurred just after the second week of classes. During the conference which followed it, I was told that my teaching was very poor, my voice was inadequate, my publications were "junk," and I had lied on my vita. When I produced a large file of international correspondence documenting the quality of my scholarship and research, I was told that this was a teaching college and research was not important. As for the alleged lie on my vita, the chairman had phoned the professional organizations I had listed and learned that one membership had been discontinued at the time of his call. Clearly, his case for "non-reappointment" was being carefully prepared.

Following is his teaching evaluation, prepared during my third week at the college:

Memorandum of Evaluation Conference, February 28, 1973
I am sorry to say that I have to give you an "unsatisfactory" rating. I think the students didn't know what you were talking about most of the time, and didn't learn much.

At the end of the film on ___ , a student asked, "What did the film mean?" He had a good point; I think you didn't do a very good job of explaining it.

Our introduction to the subject of ___ is scheduled for March 12. That is surely the appropriate time for discussion of ___ , ___ , ___ , and ___ .

One cannot expect students in the third week of the term to understand the following terms which were key words in the rest of your lecture: [11 items listed]. I think you would save your students a great deal of frustration if you would think ahead and plan your teaching for the rest of the term in accordance with the sequence of topics listed in the assignment sheets.

Your voice has a tendency to become inaudible. For example, I didn't hear a word you said during the showing of the film; I heard only a mumble. I hope this can be corrected.

Signature of Chairman: _____

Signature of Employee: _____

Under the union contract, I was entitled to write a rebuttal to this report. I tried to make it conciliatory, but firm. Following is my rebuttal of March 6, 1973.

Comments on Teaching Observation of February 20, 1973

I have carefully read your comments on my lesson of February 20. I bow to your years of experience in teaching, and in observing teachers. However, I do not agree that this lesson should have been characterized as unsatisfactory.

Of course any lesson leaves room for improvement. I had hoped for constructive criticism, discussion, and suggestions for improvement. I was therefore surprised and very concerned when you found no positive values in my lesson, and no strong points on which to build, either in your written comments or in our prior discussion. I was also concerned when you dismissed my own suggestions for improvement during our conference.

I have been a college teacher for ___ years, and my ratings have always been "very good" at the least. On that basis, I was awarded tenure at my previous institution. Therefore I find your conclusions perplexing.

The major part of this lesson was a nontechnical introduction to the topic of ___ including those events which led ___ to publish his theory. Perhaps you did not notice that I assumed no prior knowledge of the terms which you mentioned in your criticism. Incidentally, I did not mention the term ___ in my lecture at all. To choose another one of them, for example, I explained that the term ___ means ___ . I believe that any college student can understand this simple concept.

As for ___ , I was surprised and puzzled by your criticism of this term, to which the textbook also alludes. I was also surprised that you felt the students did not understand me. You left the room as the

bell rang, and therefore you did not see that several students came
forward to discuss the film and to ask questions.

I have heard you lecture, and I recognize that your classroom
techniques are superb. I believe I would have much to learn from you.
I feel there must be some valid criticisms and suggestions among all
your negative comments, but at this point I find them difficult to
identify. Perhaps our teaching styles are very different. I hope we can
soon arrive at a rapprochement on these items and begin to develop a
basis for a smooth working relationship.

Incidentally, I was surprised when you informed me of your
decision to observe me so early in the semester, especially since I
heard you say earlier that such premature observation would be
unfair.

Sincerely yours,

_____[signed]

Upon reading this, the chairman had a temper tantrum
and almost threw his lunch at me. He said the rebuttal was
full of lies. Some days later, when I examined my personal
file, I found he had annotated the rebuttal with such
remarks as: "These comments are loaded, and personally
offensive to me"; "You didn't read my memorandum right";
"So what?"; and "I found this offensive."

On March 14, the chairman handed me the expected
letter of non-reappointment, signed by himself and the
other tenured member of the department.

Dear Dr. ___ ,

I regret to inform you that your reappointment to the Department of
___ has not been approved by the Appointments Committee of the
Department, and has not been approved by the Committee on Personnel and Budget of the School of ___ . Therefore your appointment
will terminate on August 31.

Thank you for your services to the Department.

Very truly yours,

_____ [signed]

_____ [signed]

On receiving this notice, I contacted Professor K, the
president of the College Women's Committee (CWC). She
advised me to have the union file a grievance on grounds of
contractual violations and sex discrimination. She asked
me to write a detailed account of all relevant events and
discussions, starting with my initial appointment, and to
keep a detailed record of future events. She informed me of
my right to examine my personal file, and she advised me
to make a record of its contents.

When I asked to see my file, the chairman tried to stall, but I insisted on seeing it at once. Visibly upset, he removed two items from the file before handing it to me. One item was the "flippant" postcard I had sent him during my illness and the other was my rebuttal with his annotations. A few days later, on advice of Professor K, I asked to see these two items. When he refused to let me see them, I spoke in a loud, assertive voice, so that the others in the office would hear me say, "Then, you are refusing to show me material from my file." The two items were quickly surrendered to me.

Professor K helped me rewrite my vita for my appeal. Then we made an appointment to see the Dean. Professor K advised me to bring two shopping bags filled with my research and said that it did not matter which work I brought as long as it was heavy; nobody would understand my specialty anyway. I was able to fill three shopping bags.

At first, the Dean was angry because I had filed a union grievance and he refused to listen to the informal appeal. However, Professor K explained that there was a rule on timely filing, and that the grievance would be withdrawn if a settlement was made. He then agreed to discuss the matter with us.

The gist of Professor K's argument was: (a) you are firing an outstanding woman who resigned her position as a tenured full professor at another college to accept this appointment, (b) the chairman is capricious and arbitrary, and (c) the chairman is biased against women. Professor K hinted that the chancellor of the university was looking for cases of outstanding women who were in trouble. (This was a rumor then circulating among the university women.) She said that the informal appeal procedure at the college had recently been revised, and she asked for advice on the appropriate procedures to follow "prior to seeing the Chancellor." She stressed the thought that we preferred to settle this informally with the Dean, rather than by means of an outside investigation.

At the hint of sex discrimination in my case, the Dean became defensive. He pointed out that my chairman had previously employed a woman. Professor K explained that the chairman had "inherited" this tenured woman and thus had no choice but to keep her. Professor K convinced the Dean that my "non-reappointment" had been planned well in advance of my arrival at the college, and that three-bags-full of publications would embarrass the college in a woman's grievance. At this point, the Dean agreed to ask the chairman to reappoint me.

The next day the Dean called to say he had been unable to influence the chairman. A short time later, he called to say that the chairman had changed his mind and would recommend my reappointment after all. Within an hour, we sent the union's grievance officer to the Dean to formalize the conciliation. During this conference, the chairman phoned the Dean to say he had changed his mind again. With the union officer as witness to the Dean's half of the conversation, the Dean had to admit that the chairman was indeed erratic. The Dean then exerted full pressure to secure my reappointment.

Finally, on March 28, the chairman and his assistant "reconsidered" their decision as follows:

> Dear Dr. C___ :
> In recognition of the fact that so little time has elapsed since you began your teaching at A College, we have reconsidered our earlier decision not to recommend your reappointment.
>
> At a meeting of the Committee on Personnel and Budget of the School of ___ this afternoon, we recommended that you be reappointed for the academic year 1973-74, and this recommendation was accepted by the Committee.
>
> Sincerely yours,
> _____ [signed]
> _____ [signed]

Professor K warned me that this was only a partial victory, and that the chairman, like so many officials who are foiled in their nefarious plans, would try to fire me again. She told me to keep her fully informed during the next academic year. She suggested I make myself known to the faculty and administration, and that I send reprints of any new publications to the Dean. As part of this campaign, she nominated me to the College Research Committee, calling attention to my vita at a faculty meeting, and mentioning certain dramatic findings I had made.

Some members of the CWC were mobilized to help spread the word.

During that year, I received two satisfactory teaching evaluations and a second reappointment letter. However, Professor K was still not convinced that all was well; she warned me that the chairman was waiting for a chance to fire me again, this time in a more "legal" way. Unfortunately, Professor K was right. Despite an exemplary record, my annual spring evaluation for 1974 was a negative one.

On April 29, the chairman received a form letter from the Dean, requesting statistics on final grade distributions. In compiling these, the chairman noticed that the grades in my sections of the course were higher than those in his sections of this course. He flew into a rage, and accused me of being "irresponsible." He refused to acknowledge that the two student populations were very different: My students were highly motivated (pre-professional) students for whom this course was both relevant and required (for graduation and for admission to professional school); while his students were liberal-arts and open-admissions students for whom the course was a general elective. He also chose to ignore that the grade distribution in my other courses matched those of the other instructors. In a fit of pique, he scheduled my annual evaluation conference for the following day. Following is his written evaluation of May 14.

Memorandum on Annual Professional Evaluation Conference of April 30 as outlined in The Contract.

1. *Classroom Instruction and Related Activities*

    By way of review, you are in your third term of teaching at A College, and have had three classroom observations, two satisfactory, and one unsatisfactory. You have had one student evaluation in a section of the _____ course, and your file contains a tally sheet on this evaluation.

    Your grades in _____ are far too high, in comparison with my grades. I would like to find a reasonable explanation for this disparity.

    You say that many of your students get high marks even on difficult tests, and that they would have a legitimate complaint if they did not get As and Bs. You attribute their accomplishment to the fact that you provide extra review sessions beyond the

scheduled teaching hours, and that maybe you are a better teacher
than I am. You say that my students might not be able to answer
some of the questions of your exams.

According to the catalog description of the _____ course,
approved by the Curriculum Committee and the Faculty, a large
part of the subject matter of the course is [the topic of] _____.
Accordingly, in the assignment sheets that I make up each term,
and which I follow in my own teaching week by week without
falling behind, [the topic of] _____ is nearly half of the term's
work.

Let us look at the two final examinations that you have given so
far. They both consist of ten questions. In the first examination,
there is one question on _____, and that is the total content of [the
topic of] _____ in the test. In the second test, there is again one
question on _____, and this time another one on _____, and that
is the total content of _____ in the test. I have to conclude that you
have taken it upon yourself to teach a different course than the
one described in the catalog.

I picture the extra review sessions that you give the students as a
drill on a rather limited number of questions that are then given
back to the students as the questions on quizzes and final examinations: the topics are _____, _____, _____, _____, _____, and —
—— [a list of 6 topics]. Any teacher can achieve high grades and
great popularity by drilling students ahead of time on the very
questions they get on quizzes and final examinations.

The preceding observations leave me no alternative but to rate
your teaching in _____ as very unsatisfactory. I think you should
take a more responsible attitude in respect to review sessions,
quizzes, examinations, and grades, and that you should make [the
topic of] _____ a much greater and more integral part of the
course content.

2. *No administrative assignments.*

3. *Research*
   Since April you have been doing research at _____.

4. *Scholarly Writing*
   An article on _____ was published in _____, edited by _____.
   N_____ was the publisher. I do not know the date of publication
   but I know that the final proofs were sent to you in October 1973.

5. *No departmental, college, or university assignments.*

6. *No student guidance.*

7. *Course and Curriculum Development*
   You have developed a course in _____ for _____ [pre-
   professional] students. You have been corresponding with _____
   and _____ [government agencies], and some book publishers
   concerning other ideas and ways of conducting this kind of
   course.

8. *Creative works in individual's discipline*—covered elsewhere in
   this memorandum.

9. *No public or professional activities in field of specialty.*
Signature of chairman: _____
Signature of employee: _____

On May 14, the chairman also sent the following letter
to the Dean and placed a copy in my file.

Dear Dean ___ :
In response to your letter, I am writing you about the grades in the
___ course. In my sections, the tally shows 17 As, 16 Bs, 22 Cs, 3 Ds, 3
Ps, 3 Fs. I think that this is a reasonable distribution.
   I think the grades in Professor C's sections, namely 19 As, 9 Bs, 4
Cs, no Ds, No Ps, no Fs, one dropped, are completely irresponsible. I
discussed this matter with her in an annual evaluation conference on
April 30. She attributes the high grades to the fact that she provides
review sessions for the students beyond the regularly scheduled
classes and also she allows that she may be a better teacher than I
am. I think her review session are drills on a limited number of questions which are given back to the students as questions on three
quizzes and a final examination. The questions on the topic of ___ are
very limited in scope, and she hardly touches ___; for example, in her
final examination, the total content of ___ consists of one question
counting 10 percent. In the annual evaluation, I had to give her an unsatisfactory rating in her teaching of this course.
   Professor F will write to you about the grades in the other courses.
                         Yours sincerely,
                    _____ [signed]

After reading these, I called Professor K for advice,
and read the entire evaluation memo without interruption.
When I finished, there was a long silence. I knew that
Professor K was deciding what to do. Then she quietly
informed me of her decision, "We're going to break his ass."
Her decision was very reassuring.

Professor K said that everyone now knew that my
chairman was very confused and erratic. She told me that
he had been spreading a story about a woman in his
department who was "destroying all the equipment," but
the CWC members had countered this tale with the truth—
the "destroyed equipment" was a single, inexpensive fuse.
The chairman had become a college joke.

We prepared a rebuttal for this new memorandum.
This time I took it to the Dean myself, assured him I had
not approached the union, and asked for his advice.
Pleased that I had not gone to others first, the Dean read

my remarks, suggested some changes, and advised me to send it off, which I did.

Reply to Memorandum of May 14 on Annual Evaluation Conference
This is a reply to Professor A's memorandum of May 14, describing our conference of April 30, in which we discussed his perception of my performance and achievements of the past academic year.

During most of the year, our relationship had been quite pleasant. It is therefore regrettable that during the past few months Professor A has resumed his campaign of harassment.

It is certainly difficult to accurately recall statements made during oral conversations, especially when nobody is taking notes. Some of the statements attributed to me in the memo do not coincide with my recollection of the conversation. For example, I did not say I was a better teacher than Professor A, nor did I say that his students could not answer the questions on my exams. In fact, when he questioned me about these two possibilities, I said I did not know.

In his memo, Professor A concedes the following points:

1. I spend a great deal of time with my students. I hold extra voluntary classes and informal meetings with them.
2. Students rate my performance as outstanding.
3. I am popular with them.

Professor A did not include in his memo the following points I made during our conference, and in other conversations:

1. My students are required to hand in every homework assignment.
2. Incorrect work must be corrected and resubmitted.
3. I give them challenging assignments for extra credit.
4. In November, Professor A asked Professor F to observe me in a classroom situation. Professor F wrote a very favorable report. However, during this conference, Professor A said the report was not in my file, and that he knew nothing about it. I insisted that he locate it after the conference, and that he consider it in his written evaluation, which he did. That report is now in my file.
5. In December, Professor A himself observed me, and he wrote: "I rate your performance as satisfactory, and offer no criticism."

These are the facts. From these, Professor A has concluded that my teaching performance is "very unsatisfactory." His conclusion is based on a "picture" in his mind, which converts my review sessions into "drills" on the exact questions given on my tests. I do not drill students, nor do I give them test questions in advance.

During the conference, Professor A described several other fantasies he had about me. He imagined I was teaching Dr. F's large lecture class. He "pictured" the students as unruly and inattentive, and imagined my performance in the fantasy lecture as "poor." When I pointed out that this event had, in fact, never occurred, he offered to have me teach this class, so that he could observe me and verify his fantasy.

Professor A spent about a third of the 45-minute conference reviewing his first teaching evaluation of me, in which he rated me "unsatisfactory" my third week at the College. He referred to it repeatedly, relishing every detail of his negative evaluation from memory. I feel that last year's teaching evaluation should have no place in this year's annual evaluation.

During the conference, Professor A said that my examinations were too easy (although he had not seen them), and he called me "irresponsible" and "without standards." Professor A also argued that my students give me a high rating because I spend so much time with them. I believe he should find my concern for them, and their high regard for me, as evidence of my worth as a teacher.

After the conference, Professor A asked me for copies of all my exams, and spent a day studying them, and making charts. The next day he said triumphantly, "Aha! I found something. You left out [the topic of] _____. You taught only _____." By ignoring questions on my tests covering the last third of the term, Professor A "found something," i.e., just what he was looking for—a means of distorting the objective facts in order to prove his pre-conclusion.

Attached are: (1) the course outline prepared by Professor A, which I followed exactly, (2) my lecture notes for the last five weeks of the term, which include only [the topic of] _____, in agreement with the course outline, (3) my last quiz of December 1973, and (4) my final examination of January 1974.

I realize that Professor A's own work was in [the topic of] _____ and it is only natural for him to emphasize these six chapters relative to the other fourteen chapters covered in this course. Nevertheless, I followed his outline exactly. About five weeks were devoted to [the topic of] _____ in the outline [Attached Item (1)] and in my lectures [Attached Item (2)].

My quiz of December [Attached Item (3)], includes a question on each of the six chapters covered during the last five weeks of the course. (I have marked each question on this copy of the quiz with the corresponding chapter number.) Thus every aspect of [the topic of]_____ outlined by Professor A was covered in the course. Since the final exam took place so soon after this quiz, I did not think it necessary to test them again on this material.

Professor A says I gave 19 A grades in this course during the past two years. There were in fact 9 As last year, and 10 As this year. Four of the ten this year went to graduating seniors. The commencement program shows that three of these were graduated magna cum laude and the fourth cum laude. Two of the magna cum laude students received scholarships for graduate work. Thus the four graduates who received As in my course this year were honor students throughout their college careers. I have no information on the records of the other six A students for this year, since they did not graduate.

A discussion of last year's A students is not really appropriate in this year's evaluation. However, since Professor A raised the issue, I shall respond to it. Four A students of last year were graduated this year; one had magna cum laude, and two had cum laude. One received a scholarship. Only one of the four did not earn honors at graduation.

Most of my students in this course are highly motivated, pre-professional students. I have repeatedly explained to Professor A that my students earn their high grades by doing their homework thoroughly, by attending my extra voluntary classes, and by studying hard. They deserve the grades they receive.

Professor A not only deprecates my teaching, but my research as well. He called my current work "an extension" of my thesis. In fact, my thesis was written many years ago, and most of my subsequent publications are in totally different fields.

Last year Professor A delayed considering two of my articles in his annual evaluation because they were in press. These two articles have since been published, and a third article as well. In this year's evaluation, however, Professor A refused to consider the first two papers because they reflected work which was done in advance of their publication. He has also refused to consider work done elsewhere which was published after I arrived at the college.

Professor A applies different standards to other members of his department. Other members are encouraged to list works in press and works done elsewhere, including their doctoral work, among their credits for the year. If they do not include them, Professor A reminds them to do so. He praises such work publicly.

I am the only woman in the department. I am the only department member subjected to harassment. I am the only one teaching five days a week. I am the only one teaching three courses, one of which is entirely new.

In conclusion, I am the only department member whose research is deprecated, even though it is outstanding, and whose teaching is rated "very unsatisfactory" on the basis of the chairman's fantasies, and in spite of my high evaluations and extra efforts.

I protest this discriminatory treatment.

—————————————[signed]

June 12, 1974

After I sent the chairman this memorandum, the Dean offered assistance by asking for a three-way meeting with himself, the chairman, and me. At first the chairman wrote a scathing answer to my rebuttal (which he never sent, although he did place it in my file, where I found it subsequently). Then, unable to face such a meeting, the chairman decided instead to neutralize his annual evaluation by deleting most of the negative comments.

On the Dean's advice, I then revised my rebuttal to the annual evaluation to thank the chairman for rewriting it. In that way, record was made that a revision had been done, to the great discomfort of the chairman.

Response to Annual Evaluation Memorandum of May 14, 1974
Please accept my sincerest thanks for revising your May 14, 1974,
annual evaluation of my work, in the interest of harmony.

To further that interest, I think it would be appropriate for you to
consult with me and other department members in setting up
unambiguous grading standards. In view of my prior broad teaching
and administrative experience, and of my rank in the department, I
think it would also be fair and appropriate for you to ask me to
observe other members of the department in the classroom.

Sincerely,

_____ [signed]
September 15, 1975

Thus the Memo War ended as the fall semester of 1974
(my third year) began. Because the chairman had been
unable to build his case against me, because we had
established that his own conduct was arbitrary and capricious, and because the CWC had made mine a cause
célèbre, I was reappointed that October for the third time.

In November 1974, the chairman became ill and was
unable to work. He retired suddenly in December. Since he
had arranged a sabbatical leave for his assistant which
started in January (another example of the buddy system),
the position of acting chairperson was assigned to me. I
then sat on the very committee that had fired me the
preceding year.

My fight is not yet over. Even now, I often consult
with Professor K, so that we can establish a good record
for my tenure. Professor K's advice to me, and my advice to
other women in academic life is: Publish, acquire good
student and teaching evaluations, blow your own horn—
let everyone know when you make a contribution to the
college or the profession, and use the buddy system to help
other women.

During the period of most intense stress, Professor K
was completely available to me for counseling and psychological support. In the same way, she has also helped
many other women throughout the university. The only
return she ever asks for her assistance is that each woman
who receives help and survives should help at least one
other woman. Professor K believes that "sisterhood really
exists!"

In June 1975, I took over the office of President of the CWC. This relieved Professor K to handle appeals, especially those of women, throughout the university.

11

Filing a Sex Discrimination Charge with a Federal Agency

Virginia E. Pendergrass
Florida International University
Maimi

Once a woman has resolved to file a complaint, the next step is to decide with whom the complaint is to be filed. There are two main agencies investigating sex discrimination complaints. They are the Department of Labor—Wage and Hour Division and the Equal Employment Opportunity Commission. Services of both agencies are free of charge.

The Wage and Hour Division of the Department of Labor (DOL) is charged with implementing the Equal Pay Act, which requires that companies pay women the same as men for doing the same work. This is a somewhat limited mission. This agency does *not*, for example, investigate other discriminatory practices, such as the differential assignment of high-paying jobs to men and low-paying jobs to women, provided that every person assigned a particular job is paid the same salary.[1,2,3]

The Equal Employment Opportunity Commission (EEOC) administers Title VII of the Civil Rights Act of 1964, which prohibits discrimination on the basis of sex in a much broader sense than the Equal Pay Act. The EEOC can handle equal pay complaints as well as complaints relating to hiring, firing, promotions and other discriminatory employment practices.[4,5]

There are other federal agencies, such as the Department of Health, Education and Welfare, Office of Federal Contract Compliance, and the Women's Bureau, concerned with sex discrimination in employment. However, most of them do not investigate individual complaints. They also do not provide the legal evidence for a woman's suit if she files a charge in District Court, should that become necessary. These agencies may be more interested in statistical documentation of discrimination and affirmative-action programs than in resolution of individual complaints.

There are also state and local agencies which deal with discrimination.[6] Many, unfortunately, are hampered by understaffing and ineffective legislation. A woman should always be aware of these agencies as potential opportunities for redress, and use them if possible, but she should not base her hopes solely on them. She should always file with the appropriate federal agency.

WAGE AND HOUR DIVISION OF THE U.S. DEPARTMENT OF LABOR

Filing. If a woman's complaint is strictly equal pay for equal work, then she should file with the Department of Labor. The baklog of cases in DOL is relatively low, and sex and age discrimination complaints are top priority items. A woman might expect that investigation of her claim would begin within one to two months if she files with the DOL. The EEOC can also investigate equal pay complaints, but their backlog of work is larger and their process takes longer. The EEOC must first defer to the appropriate agency; if the claim is not resolved at the local level to the woman's satisfaction, EEOC will then assume jurisdiction and place her case among pending charges. The DOL can, under the Equal Pay Act, immediately and directly investigate any sex discrimination charges involving equal pay.

A woman may initiate an investigation of an equal pay complaint by writing, telephoning or personally going to the nearest Wage and Hour Division office. If the woman telephones or writes, she will later be personally interviewed or will receive a form asking for specifics. To obtain the address of the nearest DOL Wage and Hour Division office, a woman may write or call

U.S. Department of Labor
Wage and Hour Division
14 Street and Constitution Avenue
Washington, DC 20210
(202) 393-2420.

The interviewer at DOL has the prerogative of deciding whether the woman's charges "seem reasonable" and perhaps rejecting her case. If the woman is accompanied by her own lawyer, she may appear more convincing when the circumstances are unusual.

Since women will frequently have different job titles and descriptions than men even though they may perform the same duties, the DOL will have to develop evidence that the jobs are substantially similar. The complainant can assist by keeping a time chart of her own daily activities in comparison to her coworkers. This will show the percentages of time she spends in specified work activities. This information is not necessary for filing, however, since the DOL investigation should reveal the discrimination.

Investigation. After a woman has filed a complaint, the DOL will send investigators to survey all employment practices in the entire institution. The complainant is not identified. If the complainant indicates any violations of the Fair Labor Standards Act, of which the Equal Pay Act is a part, possible violations in any department will be investigated. In addition, DOL does not even inform the employer that a claim has been made; DOL occasionally conducts an industry-wide check without complaints being filed.

| APPROVED BY GAO B—180541 (RO511) Expires 1-31-81 | CHARGE OF DISCRIMINATION IMPORTANT: This form is affected by the Privacy Act of 1974; see Privacy Act Statement on reverse before completing it. | CHARGE NUMBER(S) (AGENCY USE ONLY) ☐ STATE/LOCAL AGENCY ☐ EEOC |

Equal Employment Opportunity Commission and _____
(State or Local Agency)

NAME (indicate Mr., Ms. or Mrs.)   HOME TELEPHONE NUMBER (include area code)

STREET ADDRESS

CITY, STATE, AND ZIP CODE   COUNTY

NAMED IS THE EMPLOYER, LABOR ORGANIZATION, EMPLOYMENT AGENCY, APPRENTICESHIP COMMITTEE, STATE OR LOCAL GOVERNMENT AGENCY WHO DISCRIMINATED AGAINST ME. (If more than one list below)

NAME   TELEPHONE NUMBER (include area code)

STREET ADDRESS   CITY, STATE AND ZIP CODE

NAME   TELEPHONE NUMBER (include area code)

STREET ADDRESS   CITY, STATE AND ZIP CODE

CAUSE OF DISCRIMINATION BASED ON MY (Check appropriate boxes)

☐ RACE   ☐ COLOR   ☐ SEX   ☐ RELIGION   ☐ NATIONAL ORIGIN   ☐ OTHER (Specify)

DATE MOST RECENT OR CONTINUING DISCRIMINATION TOOK PLACE (Month, day, and year)

THE PARTICULARS ARE:

I will advise the agencies if I change my address or telephone number and I will cooperate fully with them in the processing of my charge in accordance with their procedures.	NOTARY — (When necessary to meet State and Local Requirements) I swear or affirm that I have read the above charge and that it is true to the best of my knowledge, information and belief.
	SIGNATURE OF COMPLAINANT
I declare under penalty of perjury that the foregoing is true and correct.	SUBSCRIBED AND SWORN TO BEFORE ME THIS DATE (Day, month, and year)

DATE: _____ CHARGING PARTY (Signature)

EEOC FORM 5B JAN. 78   PREVIOUS EDITIONS OF ALL EEOC FORM 5'S ARE OBSOLETE AND MUST NOT BE USED

NOTICE OF NON-RETALIATION REQUIREMENT

Section 704(a) of the Civil Rights Act of 1964, as amended, states:

It shall be an unlawful employment practice for an employer to discriminate against any of his employees or applicants for employment, for an employment agency to discriminate against any individual, or for a labor organization to discriminate against any member thereof or applicant for membership because he has opposed any practice made an unlawful employment practice by this title, or because he has made a charge, testified, assisted, or participated in any manner in an investigation, proceeding, or hearing under this title.

Persons filing charges of employment discrimination are advised of this Non-Retaliation Requirement and are instructed to notify the Equal Employment Opportunity Commission if any attempt at retaliation is made.

PRIVACY ACT STATEMENT

(This form is covered by the Privacy Act of 1974, Public Law 93-579 Authority for requesting and uses of the personal data are given below.)

1. FORM NUMBER/TITLE/DATE
   EEOC Form 5B, Charge of Discrimination, Jan. 78.

2. AUTHORITY
   42 USC 2000e 5(b)

3. PRINCIPAL PURPOSE(S) The purpose of the charge, whether recorded initially on Form 5B or abstracted from a letter, is to invoke the Commission's jurisdiction.

4. ROUTINE USES. This form is used to determine the existence of facts which substantiate the Commission's jurisdiction to investigate, determine, conciliate and litigate charges of unlawful employment practices. It is also used to record information sufficient to maintain contact with the Charging Party and to direct the Commission's investigatory activity. A copy of the charge will be served upon the person against whom the charge is made.

5. WHETHER DISCLOSURE IS MANDATORY OR VOLUNTARY AND EFFECT ON INDIVIDUAL FOR NOT PROVIDING INFORMATION. Charges must be in writing, signed under penalty of perjury, setting forth the facts which give rise to the charge of employment discrimination and be signed by or on behalf of a person claiming to be aggrieved. However, use of EEOC Form 5B is not mandatory. Technical defects or omissions may be cured by amendment.

If the case boils down to a question of the employer's word against the employee, and the DOL feels there is reason for the complaint, the complainant will be asked if she wishes to be identified and testify. Her name is released only with written permission.

During the investigation, DOL will examine pay records, observe workers performing their duties, ask for testimony from workers and interview the employer. In cases where a particular infraction is difficult to prove, overall patterns of employment of men and women, including starting positions and rates of pay, may be examined over several years.

Resolution. If DOL finds no evidence of discrimination, its investigation ends. The woman may, if she chooses, pursue the charge independently, but she will not be permitted access to DOL records.

If DOL finds evidence of discrimination, conciliation will be attempted. The employer will be asked to assure future compliance and provide restitution of back pay for two years from time of settlement to *all* affected employees. (If a woman quits when she filed a complaint, and two years have passed in the investigation, she will receive no back pay.)

When conciliation is successful, the employee is asked to sign a statement accepting the settlement and waiving the right to subsequently file legal suit.

If the employer refuses to make a statement of compliance or to award back pay, DOL will consider whether the number of people and/or amount of money involved justifies the expense of a legal suit. When DOL files suit, the court can order compliance and back pay.

A woman can file suit herself through a private attorney at any time, without prior consultation with DOL, unless she has signed a waiver and accepted back pay in conciliation. If DOL refuses to investigate, or if the investigation does not produce evidence of discrimination, or if the settlement is unsatisfactory to the woman or if DOL refuses to prosecute, a woman may file suit directly.

If she does so, she is entitled to damages, court costs and other remuneration. However, she will not have access to any information gathered by DOL during any investigation they might undertake.

EQUAL EMPLOYMENT OPPORTUNITY COMMISSION

Filing. The time limit for filing a complaint is 180 days from the time the discriminatory act occurred or since all other remedies (union grievance, for example) have been exhausted. She may begin the process by telephoning, writing or personally visiting the nearest Equal Employment Opportunity Office. To obtain the address of the nearest office, the woman may write or call

Equal Employment Opportunity Commission
1800 Sixth Street, N.W.
Washington, DC 20506
(202) 343-8555.

The appropriate EEOC office will request a notarized complaint which constitutes the formal charge.

A woman can assist in the presentation of her case by putting as much as possible in writing. For example, if a woman is not being considered for a promotion for which she is qualified, she should write a memo (calm and factual, of course) in which she sets forth the reason(s) she believes she deserves the promotion. This rules out the potential future argument that the employer did not know the woman was interested in the promotion.

A woman should keep copies of all letters and memoranda dealing with her situation. If she is selling more saucepans than Joe Blow and he gets the promotion, it is helpful to have the sales record summary showing he only sold two saucepans. If postings are made of discriminatory policies or of job announcements with illegal sex qualifications, copies of those will be valuable. If a particular incident which illustrates the woman's complaint of discrimination occurs, she should go home and write a memo to keep on file stating the time, date, nature of the incident and who was listening. This should *not* be done at work, as the employer will no doubt go underground if the woman reveals the nature of the documentation.

The complainant can expect a waiting period after the charge has been filed. She should be sure to answer any

Form Approved
Budget Bureau No. 44-R0304

U.S. DEPARTMENT OF LABOR EMPLOYMENT STANDARDS ADMINISTRATION WAGE AND HOUR DIVISION	**EMPLOYMENT INFORMATION FORM** *Information furnished is confidential and will be used by the Department of Labor only*

1. PERSON SUBMITTING INFORMATION

A. Name (Print first name, middle initial, and last name)
    Mr.
    Miss
    Mrs.

B. Date

C. Telephone number:
  (Or No. where you
  can be reached)

D. Address: (Number, Street, Apt. No.)

  (City, County, State, ZIP Code)

E. Check one of these boxes
  ☐ Present employee   ☐ Former employee   ☐ Job Applicant   ☐ Other_____
    of establishment   of establishment   (Specify: relative, union, etc)

2. ESTABLISHMENT INFORMATION

A. Name of establishment

B. Telephone Number

C. Address of establishment: (Number, Street)

  (City, County, State, ZIP Code)

D. Estimate number of employees

E. Does the firm have branches? ☐ Yes ☐ No ☐ Don't know

If "Yes", name one or two locations: _____

F. Nature of establishment's business: (For example; school, farm, hospital, hotel, restaurant, shoe store, wholesale drugs, manufactures stoves, coal mine, construction, trucking, etc.)

G. If the establishment has a Federal Government or federally assisted contract, check the appropriate box(es).

  ☐ Furnishes goods   ☐ Furnishes services   ☐ Performs construction

H. Does establishment ship goods to or receive goods from other States?
  ☐ Yes ☐ No ☐ Don't know

3. EMPLOYMENT INFORMATION
(Complete A, B, C, D, E, & F if present or former employee of establishment; otherwise complete F only)

A. Period employed (month, year)

From: _____

To: _____
    (If still there, state present)

B. Date of birth if under 19 or if information concerns age discrimination

Month _____ Day _____ Year _____

C. Give your job title and describe briefly the kind of work you do

(Continue on other side)

Form WH-3 (Rev. Nov. 1974)

D. Method of payment	E. Enter in the boxes below the hours you usually work each day and each week (less time off for meals)							
$_____ per _____ (Rate) (Hour, week, month, etc.)	M	T	W	T	F	S	S	TOTAL

F.   CHECK THE APPROPRIATE BOX(ES) AND EXPLAIN BRIEFLY IN THE SPACE BELOW the employment practices which you believe violate the Wage and Hour laws. (If you need more space use an additional sheet of paper and attach it to this form.)

☐ Does not pay the minimum wage

☐ Does not pay proper overtime

☐ Men and women perform equal work but do not get equal pay

☐ Discrimination against employee or applicant (40-65 years of age) because of age

Approximate date of alleged discrimination

_____

☐ Does not pay prevailing wage determination for Federal Government or federally assisted contract

☐ Discharged employee because of wage garnishment (explain below)

☐ Excessive deduction from wages because of wage garnishment (explain below)

☐ Employs minors under minimum age for job

☐ Other (explain below)

_____

_____

_____

_____

_____

_____

_____

_____

_____

_____

_____

(NOTE: If you think it would be difficult for us to locate the establishment or where you live, give directions or attach map.)

FOR OFFICIAL USE ONLY

_____

_____

GP O 884-584

communications from the agency promptly and should keep the agency informed of her whereabouts. Failure to respond or to advise the agency within ten days of a change of address may result in automatic dropping of charges.

Investigation. When the woman's case comes up for consideration by EEOC, an investigator will notify the employer of the nature of the charges filed against him (including the name of the complainant). This agency considers it a fair part of the investigation to inform the employer fully in order to give an opportunity to respond. While harassment is illegal, subtle harassment may be difficult to prove. It is seldom, however, that an employer will take such a drastic step as firing the complainant, and if this occurs, it will be immediately remedied by EEOC or the court.

When the employer is formally notified of the nature of charges filed against him, he is also requested to supply any documents to EEOC which might bear on the investigation. These might include written copies of any policies relating to leave, overtime, hiring and firing, employee benefits and so forth. Records of payroll may also be requested. If these documents demonstrate evidence of the complaint filed, and the documents are not contested by the employer, then it will be unnecessary for the investigator to perform an on-site visit. A decision may be made in the woman's favor on the basis of documents alone. If there is no documentary evidence of discrimination, if no written policies exist or the employer presents further argument, an on-site visit may be required. The investigator will then observe the actual work situation. The investigator will attempt to obtain any further documentation that the complainant feels is relevant and will interview all witnesses whose names are provided by both the complainant *and* the employer. If the complainant feels that her witnesses will be intimidated on the work premises, interviews may be performed in another location at night.

Resolution. If the agency finds that the woman was *not* discriminated against, this could mean either the investigator was unable to find the proof required to decide in the woman's favor or the complaint did not fall within the meaning of Title VII. Unfair treatment is not always illegal under Title VII. For example, if the complainant was competing with another *woman* for promotion, and the less-qualified competitor was promoted, this *may* not be illegal under Title VII, although it might be very unfair. A woman may sue independently, even if EEOC does not find in her favor, providing that she obtains a "right to sue" letter from EEOC.

If EEOC finds in favor of the complainant, she will be issued a letter of determination stating so and bargaining for a settlement with the employer will begin. The EEOC will attempt to obtain a settlement that will "make the complainant whole." This may mean hiring with back pay, promotion with back pay or other redress. Back pay is limited to two years from time of settlement. When EEOC has obtained the best possible settlement, including a statement from the employer that discrimination will not occur in the future, the woman will be contacted again by EEOC. If the woman accepts the settlement, she must sign a waiver which prohibits any further legal action.

If conciliation is unsuccessful, and EEOC has made a finding in favor of the woman, the case is referred to one of EEOC's litigation centers. The odds are slim that a suit will be filed in the woman's behalf, because only a few cases are selected on a variety of criteria which may include legal precedent, number of people affected, amount of money involved, and so on. The woman must then decide if it is worth her own time and money to sue individually.

Right to Sue. Before a woman can file suit under Title VII, she must obtain from EEOC a "right to sue" letter. If the finding of EEOC is not in the woman's favor, if conciliation fails, *or* if 180 days have elapsed, a woman may hire a private attorney who may advise that a "right to sue" be requested. It is important to know that after requesting a "right to sue," the complainant has *only ninety days* for her attorney to file a case. A woman should *not* request a "right to sue" and then begin to look for an attorney. The time limit may expire before she is able to locate an attorney she likes, and the case will have already been lost. Occasionally, if EEOC does *not* find in favor of the woman, a "right to sue" may be included in the letter of determination. The ninety-day time limit still holds.

In summary, the recommended steps to filing are:

1. contact the local and federal agencies involved to discuss grounds, time limits and other practical matters;
2. follow through by filing a factual complaint in a timely manner;
3. assist the agency by quietly gathering as much documentation as possible that will benefit the case;
4. keep the agency advised of changes in address or prolonged vacations;
5. request a right to sue *only* after an attorney has been retained and the case is ready to be filed.

A word on conciliation. The objective of the process is redress—correcting the initial conditions which led to the complaint, including redress for remuneration lost. The object is *not* to punish the employer for his arrogance or to remediate suffering and effort of the complainant during the process of filing and pursuing the charge. While the promise of future compliance and the amount of money offered may seem puny, many complainants have turned down an offer only to end up with nothing. Consider whether the emotional and financial costs can be borne if conciliation is not successful and a court suit is pursued.

Finally, a woman doesn't have to be perfect to win a sex discrimination suit. She only has to be treated differently than males and to be disadvantaged by the treatment.

Note: In January 1979 there was a significant reorganization of EEOC and an increase in funding. Under new rules, EEOC is expected to begin processing new claims within 30 days. The additional funding will enable EEOC to file more legal cases to deal with recalcitrant employers who refuse conciliation. In addition, the agency should be using a special team of investigators to try to clear the huge backlog of cases. While it is too early to tell whether the reorganization and increases funding will enable EEOC to cary out its duties promptly and effectively, the efforts being made are encouraging.

12

A Case Herstory:
An EEOC Complaint

Anonymous

I was a secretary in the Air Force for ten years. During that time, my husband wanted to learn to fly and urged me to join the local flying club, so he could fly as my dependent. If I joined, however, I actually had to learn to fly. I was scared, but after a few times in the air, I found out I loved it. My husband didn't finish his training at that time, but I got my pilot's license.

Occasionally, I took vacation time and flew for an aerial photography team which responded to ecological disasters and provided a visual record of damages, such as flying the perimeter of an oil slick, so that it could be mapped on radar.

Meanwhile, on my job, I advanced to the highest pay scale I could and was in the same dead-end position for over five years. I actually was doing a very complex job, but the pay depended not on my job description but on the grade of my supervisor. A possibility of a full-time job with the aerial photography team came up and I quit my safe, secure job. Then there was a cutback in funding for this project, and the flying job was eliminated.

This was the first time in ten years that I was without a job; I had two years' college credit, having taken only the courses which interested me. It did not occur to me to value my various other talents such as writing, flying, supervision and photography. I finally located a job as a secretary with a manufacturing company. I was soon promoted to assistant contracts manager. In this job, I revised, modified and negotiated construction contracts and acted as an assistant to the contracts manager. The former assistant contracts manager was about twenty-three years old, had a B.A. and was considered "executive material." He didn't understand the job and was transferred from that division after six months. The company saw a golden opportunity to save money (the vice president bragged later that he could have two top-notch women executives for half of what he paid mediocre men). They had asked me to be "acting assistant contracts manager," and offered me a $50-a-month raise. The previous assistant contracts manager had been making twice my salary and was not handling the job. He did have a college degree, which was supposed to be required for the job. I still felt the offer was very unfair, because I had been doing much of the job, which was why it was offered to me now. On the other hand, I felt insecure about my lack of formal education. So I told the supervisor that I would take the position at the salary offered for six months, provided that I got a secretary to do the typing and other clerical work. If I did a good job after six months, I said I expected to be raised to the lowest salary usually paid a contracts manager.

After I took over the job, I found out that there was a lot I did not know about contract language and engineering and construction, as well as new aspects of negotiations and preparing contracts. But after six months, I felt that I was really getting the hang of the job and asked for a raise at that time. I was told that I was the highest paid woman in the company, and that I was doing very well "for a woman." I was given this answer repeatedly, as I repeatedly insisted that my salary was unfair. After a year in the job, however, I really was doing everything required of me and more. I was negotiating contracts worth over a million dollars, handling all the contract details and backing up our contracts with very tough, intricate implementation. I felt I deserved a fair salary; mind you, I still didn't think I was worth what the male made. I was still a victim of years of conditioning, and thought if I would behave in a perfectly nice and ladylike way, some day justice would come. During this process, my protests were beginning to embarrass my supervisor (who had urged my promotion in the first place) and, consequently, to create negative feelings toward me. On the other hand I was becoming increasingly frustrated and angry by what I considered was unfair treatment. Finally my boss went to his boss, the vice president (a patriarchal figure who reacted well as long as I acted subservient and "womanly"), who was angry at the idea I would think of myself as more than a secretary. He told me personally that if I were a man, I could be president of the company, because I had the brains and talent, but that it was really too bad I was a woman. I was too amazed to reply. Although I was an "outstanding asset," he just wouldn't consider giving me even the *lowest* salary which would be paid to a man in the same job. He did, however, approve another $50 raise. This clinched my case. If I had been an unsatisfactory employee, he should have fired me or at the very least refused a raise. The raise indicated that the company was satisfied with my work, but just wasn't going to pay me for it. I later asked a friend in the payroll office to get a copy of the payroll form for me. She did, but wouldn't give it to me; she said that if it came to court, she would hand over the document, and she did.

I had talked with a lawyer friend before about the legalities involved, and the lawyer said I had a good case. After the talk with the vice president, I was very unhappy and frustrated. I didn't really need the money; it was the principle. But I still didn't have the courage to file an action. I hated myself for submitting to discrimination and I hated them for discriminating against me. I literally smarted from the injustice of it.

About this time, I asked for three-weeks' leave to fly in a women's air race in Central America. As a secretary (the category the company still insisted I belonged in), I was entitled to two-weeks' vacation, and in addition I asked to take one-week advance leave with pay. (As an executive, I would have been *entitled* to three-weeks' vacation.) The company refused me the advance leave with pay, probably because of my protests. I left wondering if my job would be there when I returned and very disturbed about the entire situation. As it turned out the trip was good for me. I went for adventure and excitement, and I found it, along with a self-awareness I had previously lacked.

In the air race, we got in a very tricky situation with low clouds around a mountain pass in Southern Mexico, and at one point I knew that I was dead. Although I wanted to go into screaming panic, I kept calm and flew my way out of it, but that is the closest that I have come to dying. The next morning, my co-pilot and I got into the plane and flew on. That experience did something to me. I decided that if I could get myself together and keep flying when I was that frightened, why should I be afraid of a bunch of pompous executives? I saw the company's officials in a totally different light: When compared to that Mexican mountain they were not impressive at all. I had learned something truly amazing about myself and my perspective was forever changed.

When I returned to the company, my job was still there, although everything was in a mess. The first day back my attitude was dramatically different and they noticed. I asked my boss for the last time for a raise, and said that if no raise were forthcoming I would file suit. He asked for a few months to think about it. I filed suit the next morning with a local Equal Employment Opportunity Office and personally informed the company officials (who were violently angry and acted as though I had personally betrayed them).

Right away, other women in the company were instructed not to talk to me. When an executive was walking down the hall towards me, he would duck into an office to avoid having to talk to me. I only had one friend left; a secretary who worked directly for me was very loyal and continued to be so through what was to become a six-month ordeal.

The company took away my authority to sign letters; then the vice president requested a particular memo from me. I sent the memo. The vice president called me into his office and reprimanded me because I had signed the memo. This was one small example of daily and continuing harassment.

I would prepare contracts and then they would be held up in another office where they had to be approved. The vice president would call to reprimand me for being so lax about getting my paperwork done, and I would have to spend a half-day tracking down where the contract was being held, to get it moving again.

All this time, I was on edge every minute. Sometimes I would come home and just sit and cry for an hour before I could fix supper for my children, but on the job I bit my lip and did not show any emotion and attempted at all times to be supercapable, calm and efficient. Then I decided that was ridiculous. They were making my life completely miserable, and I might as well let them know it. One morning, I just sat at my desk and cried. I guess everyone felt a little guilty, for things eased off for a month or so. During this period the company's actions destroyed my self-confidence. I almost believed they were right and I was wrong. At that time I wished over and over that I had never raised the question of discrimination. I felt it was not worth the emotional cost to me. The reason that I did not quit up to this point was that I had been advised by the local civil rights agency that if I quit, my suit would no longer be valid. I later found out this was not true; the case would be pursued whether or not I continued to work with the company, and in fact their harassment of me was illegal and provable and later strengthened my case.

I did not definitely decide to quit until the vice president came to tell me that a secretary in another office was sick, and I would have to do her typing for six weeks, along with my own work. I refused absolutely, and he told me I would be fired if I did not obey orders. I told him I would save him the trouble, and I quit. It was just as well, because I found out later that I really would have been fired the next morning.

All the time that I was working for the company, they laughed at my suit and said that the state investigating agency was "toothless." It turned out that they were right. The state agency put my complaint on a shelf and left it there. I next took my complaint to the Department of Labor Wage and Hour Division. They first told me that I had a good case, and they would investigate. I was jubilant, then they called me back and it was like Catch-22. They said they couldn't investigate my case because it involved an administrative position, and these were not covered under the Wage and Hour Act. I said that I was not being paid as an executive, I was being paid as a secretary. But they explained that the position that I *wanted* to have was an executive position. At this point, I was in a real dilemma. There is a time limit on how long you can delay before filing a suit, and I had already wasted a lot of time with these two agencies. This had to be the low point—I felt it really had all been for nothing. Luckily, I could still file with the EEOC and by chance I came across this possibility at this time.

The day after I quit my job with the company, I was asked to resume my old job as secretary with the Air Force on a temporary basis. Although the company I resigned from gave me a negative reference, my former employer knew better—I had worked there for ten years and was outstanding all the way. I had never noticed it before, but many of the things which go with the secretarial job are humiliating, such as being responsible for making coffee. I do not even drink coffee myself, but the women always had to make the coffee and clean the coffee pot, although there were ten women and forty men in the unit. I applied for another job as affirmative-action officer with a local agency, and finally was hired. I found out afterwards that I had applied for a lower rank than men with my same qualifications. I *still* could not see myself as competent as men.

Two-and-a-half years later EEOC arranged a settlement for me of $3,500 (two-years' back pay differential). I probably could have gotten more if it had gone to court, but just to get a lawyer to handle the suit you have to come up with $2,000 or more before it even starts. I guess there are a few lawyers who will take it on a contingency fee, but the reason that they do not like to do it is that Title VII suits involve a huge amount of research and rewards are slim. Of course, the *companies* have lawyers who do nothing else full time, yet make a bundle.

Even after two years away from the company, I just felt great hostility whenever I thought about the way they treated me. All of the people who had treated me unfairly were fired. I am not usually vengeful, but I was in this case. I never felt such anger and hostility; usually I am easy-going and cheerful. Everyone told me I was wrong, even my own relatives. At least my husband and children stood up for me or I never could have made it (and the whole thing was an ordeal for them too). Before the suit everyone, men and women, had thought well of me. Then, after the suit, everyone criticized me—women, too. After a while, I just did not even know who I was anymore. There was *no* justice and the way that I was treated was *wrong*. I felt at first that I was not good enough and did not have the education I should have, but I found out that my skills qualified me very well for the job, and a person did not have to have a college degree to do it.

One of the reasons that I sought the job as an affirmative-action officer is that I felt no person should ever have to experience what I went through. Until the day the settlement was in my hands I was very tense whenever the subject was raised. This tension did not ease until the resolution of the charge, almost three years later. At times I felt I was not going to make it. My religious faith and the loyal support of my husband and children enabled me to endure the experience and come out stronger for it. I do not know how a woman alone would be able to cope, especially if her family is financially dependent upon her. However, at the end I can honestly say it was worth it. I changed profoundly and I like the new me much better. I could never go back to the role I was playing before this occurred (hiding competence and intelligence; being "non-threatening" and always feminine). Whenever I see a woman win her fight I feel—and say: "Right on, sister! *It's worth it!*"

13

Legal Suits

Joan Joesting   and Roberta Fulton Fox
Monroe County Schools   *Gold and Fox, P.A.*
Key West, Florida   *Miami, Florida*

The first steps which must successfully be negotiated in filing a sex discrimination suit may actually be accomplished, for better or worse, before the complainant has even conceived of suing. Other channels of remediation must be exhausted before suing, and the process of exhausting these resources may bear greatly on the suit finally filed.

Most organizational handbooks describe the grievance procedures that a woman must complete before appealing to outside agencies or filing in court. Civil service regulations for local, state and federal employees also specify grievance procedures. If these procedures are not properly satisfied, the incipient legal suit may be returned to the agency/institution or dismissed. In order to assure that a good basis for legal suit is laid, any woman initiating a grievance should treat the matter *as if* she will file suit; a decision not to file can, of course, be made later. When a woman confronts any administrator, she should have witnesses with her, since unconfirmed verbal statements can easily be denied in court. During the initial grievance procedure, the administrator may learn much about how to present his/her case and real reasons for administrative actions may be successfully obscured in court without documentation. The best witness, of course, is the complainant's lawyer, but other experienced friends may also serve. In addition, the complainant should attempt to get everything in writing.

When the grievance procedure has been exhausted, the complainant may then turn to local and state laws prohibiting sex discrimination. For a list of state laws prohibiting sex discrimination, see Ross.[1] One should be aware that in some enlightened municipalities, local ordinances may actually exceed federal and state regulations, or state regulations may be more comprehensive than federal legislation. In lieu of good local or state legislation, federal legislation exists.

GOVERNMENT CONTRACT LEGISLATION

One *potentially* powerful piece of legislation for women is Executive Order 11246, amended by Executive Order 11375. The amended Executive Order became effective in October 1967; it prohibits discrimination in employment (hiring, salaries, fringe benefits, training and other conditions of employment) on the basis of sex, race, color, religion or national origin. If a contractor does not comply, contracts may be canceled, terminated or suspended; and the contractor may become ineligible for further contracts. The legislation covered all employees of institutions with federal contracts of over $10,000. The time limit for filing a complaint is 180 days. The Secretary of Labor is responsible for administering provisions for nondiscrimination in government contracts. Unfortunately, this legislation is not frequently used in women's behalf. For further information, see Eastwood.[2]

TITLE VII OF THE CIVIL RIGHTS ACT

As amended in 1972, Title VII prohibits discrimination by private employers with 25 or more employees, in employment agencies and labor organizations. It is enforced by EEOC, and the time limit for filing a complaint is 180 days.[3]

The name of the woman filing a complaint is given to the employing institution, and although harassment is prohibited, it is difficult to prove.

EQUAL PAY ACT

Another law protecting women is the Equal Pay Act of 1963, as amended by the Education Amendments of 1972, which became effective in July 1972. It covers all institutions without exemptions and prohibits discrimination in salaries, including almost all fringe benefits. The Equal Pay Act is enforced by the Wage and Hour Division of the Employment Standards Administration of the Department of Labor. Although women holding jobs equivalent to men are frequently paid less,[4] this Act does not help women who are experiencing difficulties in hiring and promotion rather than equivalent pay.

PUBLIC HEALTH SERVICE ACT

Titles VII and VIII of the Public Health Service Act cover all institutions receiving or benefiting from a grant, loan guarantee or university subsidy to health personnel training programs or receiving a contract under Title VII or VIII of the Public Health Service Act. These laws prohibit discrimination in admission of students on the basis of sex and discrimination in employment practices relating to employees working directly with applicants or students in the program. This law became effective November 1971.

All of this legislation is summarized in a brochure prepared by the American Association of American Colleges Project on the Status of Education of Women entitled "Federal Laws and Regulations concerning Sex Discrimination in Educational Institutions."[5]

FINDING A LAWYER

In the 1960s, some women claimed finding a spouse with whom to live happily ever after was easier than finding a lawyer sensitive to sex discrimination. Few lawyers were experienced or interested in pursuing such cases. This lack of experience and/or interest was reflected in demands for retainers or prepayment of fees which prohibited most women from using their services. Since some significant cases have been won, and large settlements *including lawyers' fees* have been obtained, this specialty is now more common. In addition, consciousness-raising in the women's movement has had a profound effect on all professional women, including lawyers, and there is substantial interest among women lawyers in sex discrimination legislation and litigation. A woman contemplating a legal suit today can probably find, with a little searching, a well-qualified lawyer with her/his head in the right place on women's issues. Avenues that a woman might investigate to locate a sympathetic, qualified lawyer are: local feminist organizations, local bar associations' lists of lawyers specializing in sex discrimination cases, old newspaper accounts of sex discrimination suits in the area, union representatives with experience in sex discrimination grievances and women who have filed suits themselves. The American Civil Liberties Union, the National Organization for Women Legal Defense Fund and other civil rights organizations are *unlikely* to pick up a case unless it will have consequences beyond the effect on the litigant, but don't neglect to ask.

The potential litigant should arrange an interview with the lawyer to whom she is referred to check out the views and style of the lawyer and her own feelings about working with this person. Since lawyers' fees are ordered by the court in successful cases, and since some precedent for such litigation has been established, there will be some lawyers with poor attitudes or qualifications who may attempt to attract clients in this area simply because it can be profitable.

While the lawyer, in the first interview, should not be overwhelmingly discouraging, a frank, open lawyer may not seem to the potential litigant to be excessively encouraging, either. The following kinds of information should not be interpreted by the woman as being negative toward sex discrimination cases: She should expect to be told that her case, justified though it may be, will be difficult to prove, that harassment may occur, that the employer will attempt to offer minor concessions to "co-opt" the litigant, that the case will require time and money, that judges and juries are just as likely to be sexist as are employers and that if she loses the case, she will be looking for a new job. Some lawyers feel that if the woman is not angry or determined enough to proceed in the face of this realistic appraisal, she is not likely to succeed in her suit.

The lawyer should *not* require a retainer before taking the case, or prepayment of fees, since a successful conclusion to the case will result in the lawyer's fees being ordered by the court, separate from and in addition to any settlement obtained by the woman herself. If the lawyer asks for retainer or prepayment of fees, the woman should conclude that either her case does not appear promising (i.e., the case will probably lose and no fees will be awarded by the court) or that the lawyer is not particularly interested in sex discrimination litigation as part of her/his practice.

Other observations which might help the woman to judge whether this lawyer will be appropriate for her case are: the status of women in the law firm (Are women attorneys in research roles only? Are secretaries treated courteously?); and the readiness with which the lawyer grasps feelings of the woman towards colleagues' remarks about her attractiveness, home responsibilities, marital status and other nonwork-related characteristics. Most lawyers, sexist or not, are quite prepared to give acceptable answers to such overt questions as opinion on the Equal Rights Amendment, so ploys such as these will not be informative.

Costs and Fees

There are two kinds of expenses which should be anticipated by the potential litigant: costs and fees. Costs may begin as soon as the lawyer takes the case and will be substantial. Costs do *not* include any payment to the lawyer for professional time expended in preparing the case or representing the litigant. Costs include such items as court filing fees, witness fees, transcript fees and so forth. A listing of approximate costs for a *well-prepared* case in a southeast area include:

10 depositions @ $30 ea. for court reporter	$ 300
5 transcripts of important depositions @ $120-200 ea.	800
10 supoenas for witnesses,including $20 fee for witness and $7.50 for service	275
1 court filing fee	19
1 notification of defendant (mileage plus service fee)	10
1 court reporter for preliminary hearings @ $30 per day	30
1 court reporter at trial @ $100 per day	300
	$1,734

A woman might anticipate costs, not including professional fees for the attorney(s), in a case of average complexity in the southeast area to run about $1,700-$2,000. Costs vary depending upon area of the United States in which the case is filed. The client must be able to pay these costs; most lawyers would *not* be willing to pay costs for the client in the expectation of being reimbursed from the settlement obtained for the client.

Naturally, the employer may be able to call upon substantial financial resources, especially if the company is large and the case might set a precedent affecting a large number of employees. If so, the number of depositions, copies of records and other needs for preparatory materials may become very great and the funds necessary for costs alone can skyrocket. Women should *not* expect to receive much financial help from other people or organizations; feminist groups are notorious for being long on sympathy and short on contributions of cash.

This does *not* mean that a woman cannot file suit if she has little money. It does mean that the case will have to be presented within the financial limitations of the woman's pocketbook. If a woman has $250, there are lawyers who will take the case and use the $250 for essentials such as filing fees and other absolutely necessary court costs. Depositions, which represent a major expense, will be avoided whenever possible. The problem with this is that without depositions, the woman's lawyer cannot be certain until the day of court exactly what witnesses will say; even the woman's own friends may become frightened at the prospect of testifying in court and tone down their remarks or change their testimony from that promised. Without pressure of subpoenas and depositions, most of the employers' witnesses will not speak to the woman's attorney at all.

As mentioned before, the attorney's fees will be ordered paid by the employer in court if the litigation is successful. This award is separate from the settlement achieved by the litigant and will not be deducted from her award. Most lawyers will request that the woman sign an agreement which guarantees fees if the woman settles out of court. This prohibits the client from cutting out the attorney in a pre-trial settlement with the employer after the attorney has expended substantial effcrt in building a case strong enough to coerce the employer into negotiating. This agreement should *not* preclude a pre-trial settlement, nor should the client lose complete autonomy in deciding whether or not to accept a negotiated settlement. The potential litigant should read carefully and fully understand the purpose and terms of the agreement.

PROGRESS OF THE CASE

Lawyers recommend that the woman open the legal relationship before they file a complaint with the appropriate government agency. The lawyer can assist in writing up the charge formally lodged with the government agency, so that information most likely to succeed is clearly included in the charge. The lawyer can also write letters to the agency, call the investigator assigned to the case and go to the government office if necessary to hassle the case along through the bureaucratic channels. All of this can be done without the aid of a lawyer, but agency representatives have unofficially stated that a complaint is likely to be processed more speedily and carefully if an informed critic is following up on their performance.

In any case, the lawyer will probably insist that the woman first process her complaint through the proper government agency (even though this is not necessary in an equal pay complaint), and unless the agency dallies inordinately in processing the complaint, she/he will wait to begin private action until a determination has been made by the agency. If a favorable determination is returned, but no settlement was reached, the lawyer may also wait a period of time to see if the agency's legal department will file charges in behalf of the woman.

If no satisfaction is received through agency channels or if the agency does not respond within a reasonable (or unreasonable) amount of time, the lawyer may then file private suit. This will require a "right to sue" letter from EEOC, if that agency is involved. **A case must be filed within ninety days after a "right to sue" letter is issued**. The employer has twenty days to respond to the charges filed by the woman's lawyer, at which time a federal court date is set. During the time between the employer's response and the court date, the discovery procedure takes place, in which witnesses are interviewed and depositions taken, records subpeonaed and files from the government agency requested. It happens occasionally that due to illness or other business, one of the parties is unable to keep the original court date which may lead to some further delay. The case will usually be heard in less than a week, once the case reaches court, and a decision is delivered immediately by the judge or jury.

A typical timetable for a case originally processed by EEOC (the most lengthy procedure) might read as follows:

Investigation by local agency to which EEOC defers	60 days
EEOC investigation allowance before each of the "right to sue" letters not issued	180 days
(Conciliation by EEOC)	(60-360 days)
Filing of private suit	90 days
Response of employer	20 days
Discovery procedure	90-180 days
(Postponement of pre-trial hearings)	(60-180 days)
Federal court apppearance	1-15 days

A woman might reasonably expect, therefore, to wait for a determination in her case from one to three years if trial is required. During this time, the lawyer will probably be somewhat annoyed if the woman frequently calls for information or supportive counseling, since she/he is unlikely to see this as her/his role.

The settlement to which a woman is entitled if she wins the suit are two years' back pay differential and/or promotion to job refused or similar job; and lawyers' fees and court costs. She is not entitled to punitive damages or reimbursement for suffering or other considerations.

WINNING

Apparently, the thing a woman must do best to win her case is wait. There are, however, some more active steps a woman might take to appear strong in court. If a woman is harassed, ignored or sabotaged at work, this should be reported to the lawyer. If the harassment is subtle and the lawyers' persuasiveness does not improve the situation, the harassment will probably be hard to stop, although it is illegal. Nevertheless, suggestions of harassment during the course of the suit may produce an undesirable picture of the employer during the actual court appearance.

If the woman is actually fired, she may immediately file with EEOC to obtain an injunction against the employer. A litigant may also quit her job, although this may lead to charges by the employer that the woman was a troublemaker and didn't like the job anyway. However a woman might become unemployed, she has a duty to seek other employment and she will be entitled *only* to the difference in pay between her new employment and her legitimate salary with her original employer. If the woman does not seek employment, she will lose her case.

If the woman works where employees are unionized and if there is any hope of support from the union, she should immediately investigate union representation in her case. Even if she opts for a private lawyer rather than union representation, the union can be very influential in assisting the woman's attorney by providing numerical support and statistical information.

Finally, a woman should be aware that any behavior which might be considered to interfere with efficient job performance under ordinary circumstances (drug and alcohol use, medical conditions, poor motivation to continue in the job) will be used by the employer as a basis for explaining discriminatory practices. Drug and alcohol use would best be avoided, medical conditions kept under cover (don't use medical coverage provided by employer which requires reporting of diagnoses) and consideration of more attractive job offers not discussed with employers or coworkers.

Seeking additional training in the interim may be either helpful or harmful. If the woman seeks training which qualifies her for a different job than she was seeking, she will be portrayed again as a troublemaker and not really interested in the employment causing the complaint. If she seeks training which will make her a more valuable employee, however, she will be seen as highly motivated to perform the contested job.

The decision to file a legal suit is not impulsively made. Most women sue because they need more money or need a job. They have usually tried negotiations, pleading, persuasion and every other avenue open to them. Most women are very anxious about the consequences of suing.

The economic, emotional, intellectual and physical drain on women and their families cannot be exaggerated. However, the woman who sues does not necessarily become unemployable. To some extent, a woman may grow from the disciplined gathering and relaying of facts and from learning to handle rejection and other punishing experiences.

Women who run away from sex discrimination instead of running to court don't get to run anything. In addition, an immediate reinforcer is the observation that if one woman files a suit, another woman will get hired.

Although legal suits require a long-term commitment of months or years and of money, family responsibility and emotional turmoil, they need not be devastating. The litigant, and women who follow, may be benefited tremendously.

14

A Case Herstory:
A Legal Suit*

Victoria L. Eslinger
Eslinger·& Knowles
Columbia, South Carolina

As a first-year law student, I wanted to be employed as a senate page with the state legislature. Senate pages run errands for the senators, occasionally make phone calls, bring cokes, look up bills and so forth. The jobs were desirable for a number of reasons: the pay was good (up to $10 an hour); the work schedule was flexible (one could work any twelve hours per week one chose and was allowed to bring books and study); the job allowed one to observe the legislative process first-hand and to get to know many of the lawyer-legislators who could be helpful later. Many of the present senators had been senate pages. One has to be appointed by at least one senator from her/his district. At the time I was not aware that women were not allowed to be pages.

One of the senators from my district (and later all four of them) sponsored me and I was told to go to the senate to pick up my application. At the senate chambers, a woman

---

*Eslinger v. Thomas, 476 F2d 225 (4th cir 1973).

told me that women could not hold the position of senate page. When I insisted that she give me an application, she sent me to the clerk of the senate. The clerk informed me that the job was not suitable for women because of occasional late hours due to filibusters, because pages had close contact with the senators, and further because in all of his years as clerk he had not hired a female and would retire before he did. Then he told me that women would reduce the dignity of the senate by their presence and that senators "would hire their girlfriends." He said he admired a "girl" with spunk but that I would have to realize that there were certain things women just could not do.

I told him that I was a law student and that I didn't think he had the right to deny my application for employment. I left the chambers contemplating suit. There was one other woman in my law class who had been appointed from another county and who was refused employment. We had both approached the lieutenant governor and were given the run-around. He informed us that he had no appointments but that he agreed with the principle of appointing females. The male who was waiting to see him after us entered his office and exited a few minutes later saying that the lieutenant governor had just appointed him page.

I held off suing initially because certain politicians asked me to wait until they introduced a bill to allow for the hiring of females. The legislature did not pass it. I then began the search for a lawyer. I went to the American Civil Liberties Union; the attorney informed me that the case was "clear-cut" and agreed to take the case free. The organization subsequently handled the case up to the Circuit Court of Appeals.

I asked the other woman in my law class to join me as a named plaintiff as the matter was to be a class action. She refused because she was contemplating entering politics after graduation. She said that she could not take the chance of bad publicity from filing a lawsuit against the state senate. She did give good testimony and was in some of the news stories when it became apparent that the only press was good press.

After I decided to file suit we applied to the court for a Temporary Restraining Order (TRO) asking that the legislature be restrained from discriminating while the matter was at trial. It took the court *three months* to act on the TRO. During the hearing on the TRO, arguments were raised which surfaced continually during the course of the trial hearings. One major argument was that during filibusters, senators sometimes go to hotel rooms to sleep and have to be awakened by pages. Of course, no one objected to the idea of women senators being awakened by male pages (there was not a woman senator at the time, but there had been one in the past). The federal judge, from the bench, suggested that the reason I wanted to be a page was to have the opportunity to get in senators' hotel rooms at night. Everyone in the courtroom gasped, including the court reporter. I was floored and speechless. The press reported the remark in all of the papers—it is against the law in this state to insult a woman's chastity—and the citizens were upset. I got a great deal of support. Even the state newspaper ran an editorial which asked the judge to apologize. Finally, the judge called us back and apologized. Some apology; it was evident that it was not voluntary. Federal judges are immune to actions for their conduct while on the bench so there was nothing for me to do. The TRO was denied.

Just prior to the hearing on the merits at the trial level (before appeal was taken), the legislature, in an attempt to moot the case, passed legislation allowing women to work in the senate and house as legislative aides and committee attendants. The duties were spelled out (we would not be allowed to go to senators' hotel rooms at night), and we had to have a parent or husband's consent to take the job. The legislature's intent was so obvious and the conditions to employment so degrading that I refused to apply for such a position. I forget to mention that initially after my indication to the senate that I would not fade into the woodwork, the clerk suggested that I accept employment as a tour guide in the state house, an exciting job.

Meanwhile, the senate had a closed session to discuss

their action on the matter. They decided that they would defend the suit rather than hire women and one of the senators defended, along with the state attorney general's office. In other words, the suit was defended at the expense of the taxpayers.

At the trial level, the testimony centered on the fact that women would be unsuited to working late at night. We would have to carry large amounts of money, go into senators' hotel rooms at night, have to pack suitcases, carry their car keys and drive their automobiles. One senator was upset that the method of summoning a page to a senator was by raising the hands and clapping. ("Your Honor, would you want somebody to call your daughter by clapping their hands?") Many of my classmates who were pages were called as witnesses. They testified that they did not want to work with women and that they would not want their sisters to be pages. Young women employed in the new position of legislative aide testified that they did not feel discriminated against, that they realized that the senate had their best interests in mind, and that they would be upset if nobody undertook their protection by forbidding them to work at night. At times the testimony was so absurd that the courtroom was filled with giggles, which the judge did not appreciate.

We won the suit in 1973 just prior to final exams of my senior year. I decided not to take the job because I would only be employed three weeks or so.

The decision to file suit was difficult—I did not know what the reaction would be. The other woman in my class would not join me in the suit because of possible pressure; my father was angry. All of the circuit judges in the state were former legislators; I knew that some of the legislators that I would be suing might be judges when I finished school. I knew that in the practice of law I would have to work with them. All of these factors made the outcome unpredictable in terms of my life and future career. I was worried, but every time I thought of the gross injustice and the treatment due to my class rather than my capabilities, I got angrier. Principle won out.

My mother was very supportive in the whole matter. My father, who is very conservative legally and politically, was quite upset. He felt that the senate should not discriminate but if they did, then it was their right. He was greatly concerned with the fact that the American Civil Liberties Union was handling the case and often made remarks as to their Commie leftist background.

The reaction of my fellow law students and professors was amazing. Professors made snide comments in class; if I was not present, the professor might send somebody into the hall to "page me." The students were hostile to the suit and to all of the women law students. It is hard to say if all of the hostility was due directly to the suit. We women refused to sit complacently while professors made women the butt of the joke. The law library at one time refused to hire women students because we "couldn't lift the books"; my second year in law school, we changed their attitudes. I also became involved in the national abortion rights movement (the suit opened my eyes to the condition of women and the legal/social problems we face as a class) and was quite outspoken on the matter. Abortion is not very popular as an issue in this state and was even less so during 1972. I imagine some of the hostility was generated by these positions.

I got a lot of support from the women in the law school and especially from the press. I do believe that the support of the press made the decision much easier for me as most of the citizens were sympathetic. Little old ladies in tennis shoes from all over the state wrote to me. The attention of the press made it difficult for any abuse to take place, since they were interested in the matter and would have listened if I had brought charges of other misconduct.

In the next two law classes, more women were admitted. In my third year, the women invited the National Conference of Women in the Law to meet at our school, and asked for $600 for Martha Griffiths as speaker. It was presented to the law school for a vote. The freshman class was in favor, the junior class split about fifty-fifty, and the senior class (my class) was not in favor. The overall vote was just in favor and we did invite her. The women who are entering now think the problem is solved, and are not as involved, because they don't see the open hostility. I am in an all-women law firm now, and we have been told we won't make it—not because we're no good, but because there is no man in the firm. So I guess attitudes are the same as when suit was filed.

Although I may not be very well liked, I think I forced respect.

15

Sex Discrimination: Special Problems of Black Women

Endilee P. Bush
Florida Atlantic University
Boca Raton

Black women face both "isms"—racism and sexism; this double jeopardy poses a terrific dilemma for them. It is often difficult for Black women to decide which of the two evils causes them most suffering, which of the two they must spend their limited time and energy to eradicate.

Statistics reveal that the Black woman is the greatest victim of both race and sex discrimination. It is true that the average woman's wage is less than that of the average male, but the annual wage of the Black woman is substantially less than the three groups: Black men, white women and white men. Seventy-eight percent of all working Black women are in "less skilled" service jobs (service workers, domestics and operatives) compared with 39 percent of working white women at this level.[1] In addition, only a small percentage of female professional, technical and kindred workers are Black women and a large percentage of those are teachers in elementary and secondary schools.[2]

While the Black woman has the most reason to protest discrimination in employment and supposedly has the broadest protection under law, the process of protest is also loneliest for her. Not only must the Black woman face the same rejection, harassment, retaliation from employers and/or colleagues any woman faces in pursuing a sex discrimination action, but she must also contend with criticism and lack of understanding on the part of kindred minority groups who should most sympathize—white women and Black men.

ISOLATION IN THE BLACK COMMUNITY

Black men have demonstrated that they are subject to the same sexist influences prevalent in the larger society, and in addition may also have incorporated into their own thinking racist attitudes reflected in their treatment of their women. Granted, Black men are not in a position to alter the societal status of Black women, but they can and must act to change those things which are within their power. One important thing that Black men can do, and often don't, is to show respect for the Black women. Abbey Lincoln[3] points out that "When the white man likes 'colored girls' his woman (the white woman) is the last to know about it. When the Black man 'likes white girls' his woman (the Black woman) is the first to know. . . ."

The Black woman has been celebrated in history and literature (the recent *Autobiography of Miss Jane Pittman* is an example) as the savior of the Black race. When the Black man walked or was driven away, she was the one who had to raise the children and had to make it one way or another. The Black woman had to be "frighteningly" strong in order for Black Americans to survive.[4] This very strength which supposedly sustained the Black race, however, is now viewed by the Black man as evil. The Black woman is accused of being too oriented toward the middle-class, too threatening, too castrating, too independent and impatient, too ambitious and contemptuous, too sexually inhibited and unimaginative. Other myths Black men

express are that Black women are not supportive and are
unwilling to submerge their interests for Black men's.

This point of view is aired in an interview with a
Black man who made it:

> I'm a dude who doesn't like a woman who competes with her man.
> As a rule Black women are more competitive than white women in
> most things, even sex, and I understand why. Anybody who knows
> Black history knows how Black women were forced to be aggressive
> in order to survive and help their men and children survive. Competi-
> tion is just built into them. White women didn't have to compete so
> hard, so they're usually more willing to let their men take complete
> charge. It so happens that I'm a take-charge man all the way.[5]

The Black woman, who developed independence through
necessity, is condemned by the Black man.

As Black men gain better-paying jobs and higher
status, they tend to act and think as sexist as white men
do. In addition to the typical suppression of women by a
sexist society, Black men in a racist society who have
hang-ups about their own self-worth and accomplishments may try to use Black women to demonstrate their
own status. They may attempt to make Black women
submissive supporters of their own success, and restrict
their partners' growth to avoid competition. They may
discourage their mates from seeking jobs which would
allow their women to earn more than they do, or attend
college at nights, or to work toward higher degrees that
would put their women at a level higher than the one they
hold.

Some Black men resort to violence and dehumanizing
tactics in order to dominate the marital relationship and
compensate for their own weaknesses. It has been suggested that this type of behavior on the part of a Black man
is a response to the stereotype of the "castrating Black
woman." Educated Black men have a responsibility to re-
examine the stereotypes and repudiate them with facts.
Black women have a responsibility to resist domination
and manipulation at all costs; to allow themselves to be
subordinated to Black men in this manner can be a terrific
waste of Black talent and creativity which the race can ill
afford.

Another attitude that Black men may maintain in conflict with the needs of Black women is the expectation that Black women should produce as many children as possible to protect Blacks from genocide. Black women are rejecting this point of view, recognizing that the emotional and physical demands of producing and caring for many children may be very destructive of the individual Black woman, although there is grave concern among Black women as well as men about sterilization and birth control as a racist program.[6,7]

Such diverse attitudes, feelings, needs, antagonisms and expectations within the Black community mean that the Black woman who embarks upon a serious career, and who will therefore ultimately be involved in sex discrimination and protest in the employment sector, is also adrift at home. A vision of the educated, ambitious Black woman is provided by Brooks:

> Maude, who went to college,
> is a thin brown mouse.
> She is living all alone
> In this old house.*

ISOLATION FROM WHITE WOMEN

It is significant to note that sexism and racism were created and are maintained by the same mentality. The basic assumption is the same: that one group was born to lead and the other to follow. To sustain and reinforce this assumption, myths were created. The superordinate-subordinate relationships were established. Many of the stereotypes of Blacks and women are similar. For example, they are both said to be irrational, emotional, passive, dependent and supportive. There are beliefs about their place in society, beliefs about their leadership ability, beliefs about their inferiority. White women, unfortunately, have beeen slow to develop genuine appeciation of these similarities between racism and sexism.[9]

---

*Last stanza from "Sadie and Maude" in *The World of Gwendolyn Brooks* by Gwendolyn Brooks. Copyright 1944 by Gwendolyn Brooks Blakely. Reprinted by permission of Harper & Row, Publishers, Inc.

Many Black men perceive the Black woman as "liberated." Black women might be liberated from many of the basic necessities of life such as family life, love and respect from Black men, meaningful work, the basic necessities and comforts of ordinary existence. This type of liberation has nothing in common with the women's liberation movement, the civil rights movement, or freedom. Black women have been forced to stand on their own two feet and to stand alone.

Despite the negative treatment received from Black men, many Black women are hesitant to join the women's liberation movement. Foster[10] doubted that a coalition of Black and white women would be democratic after the revolution. She argues that Blacks find it difficult to overlook the fact that the so-called oppressed white women have been the causes of the "loss of Emmett Till, the Scottsboro boys, and countless sons, husbands, and lovers of Black women." It is difficult also, according to Foster, to ignore the fact that white mothers assaulted and obstructed the sons and daughters of Black mothers at "dozens of Little Rocks." Racism is directed toward Black women as well as Black men, by white women as well as white men.

The opposite of this view is also true. The elimination of racism does not guarantee the equal treatment of Black women by men—Black or white. It appears that the Black woman has little choice. The ills of sexism—lack of child care for working mothers, rape (by Black and white men), forced sterilization, nonrepresentation or underrepresentation in significant job categories and politically, poverty—are only compounded by the ills of racism. The plight of the Black woman makes it necessary for her to support both movements. While it is true that there are some concerns common to Black women and not to white women which might mandate an all-Black-women organization, there is no need for this subgroup to remain totally separate from the larger group of women. Black and white women have many problems in common which make it crucially important to put the past behind them.

Black and white women must recognize that a major

roadblock to progress in employment is the "divide and conquer" technique. Minorities and women constitute groups with equal rights which should equally be enforced. It is divisive and meaningless when leaders of lily-white, all-male boards, who have not taken their responsibility seriously, say, "The thrust is on minorities this year" or "The thrust is on hiring women this year." Until the goal of full equality of opportunity for everyone is achieved, then the thrust will be on Blacks, women, Chicanos, American Indians and every other discriminated group every year, if the law is to have any meaning. There is not one job to be divided between women and other minorities; there are many jobs for well-qualified people of all minority groups. For women to compete with other minorities is for women to relieve sexist, white males of their burden—"keeping them in their place." The competing minorities will keep each other disorganized and demoralized.[11]

Many Black women will find it difficult to forget the past and work harmoniously with white women, but they must realize that just as Black men (and women) believed the myths and stereotypes of racism and sexism, so did white women. The Black woman, at the bottom of the heap of humanity, must select rational strategies for the elimination of both racism and sexism, putting aside blame and unforgiveness. The white woman must respond by recognizing the double burden of the Black woman and by giving extra understanding and support during discrimination actions.

16

A Case Herstory: Race Discrimination

Dorothy Thorne
Cleveland State University
Ohio

Editor's Note: Since the loyalties of minority women may be split, and since race discrimination as a basis for suit is more firmly established than sex, many minority women will elect to file suit on the basis of race and not sex. Here is perhaps the one instance when the opportunities of minority women are more rather than less. The following is an example of a woman who chose to file a discrimination suit on the basis of race rather than sex.

When I filed the charge of employment discrimination in July 1973, it wasn't the first experience I had had with discrimination. I had a lifetime of experience. But this time I just said, "It's enough." I decided I wouldn't let it happen anymore.

I worked in social work agencies for twenty years as a practitioner, supervisor and administrator. While I was working in a poverty program, one of my responsibilities was training paraprofessionals. We always found that workers with a B.A. in another field needed practical *skills* they didn't get in school. I also became convinced that if workers liked people, and had a sincere desire to help others, they didn't need a Ph.D.—skills could be taught.

Because of this experience, I felt I had something special to impart and was interested in a teaching job. About this time (1970), an undergraduate social work program was developing at a new university in our downtown urban area. I was very excited about the prospect of helping to develop a teaching program in a new school open to new ideas. I applied for a position in March 1970; I was told there were no jobs but that my resume would be "kept on file." In 1973, I asked again, and discovered that in the meantime six people had been hired but there was "no opening at this time." Three months later I knew a position was open and tried to make an appointment for an interview.

My calls were not returned for two months. When I finally got a response, I was told that I was "almost too late" and that I should submit a new resume for the job of field coordinator. Since I had worked in agencies in the community for years, this was an ideal job for me.

On Thursday, I sent my resume. The next Tuesday, the department chair asked for an interview within twenty-four hours. Although I had now tried for months to get information about a job at X, they still had no job description. I felt very frustrated about an interview on such short notice with no job description but went anyway.

I was scheduled for further interviews with all faculty three to four days later (Monday), still with no job description. I finally got the job description during the faculty interview when I refused to go further without it. The total investigation of my references consisted of one telephone call which was not returned until after the interviews. On Friday of the same week, I received a rejection.

The interviewing and checking of my credentials was casual and indifferent. I am sure the only reason I was interviewed at all was a perfunctory way of conforming to the university's affirmative-action program. The rejection was anticlimactic; I knew the answer as soon as I was interviewed.

I called to investigate the decision. I was the only black candidate. Some of the faculty members had wanted to hire me but they decided on an M.S.W. with only five years' experience (compared to my twenty) who was known to the faculty.

I promptly filed with EEOC. They had to take the complaint to the state first, where nothing happened for sixty days. On the sixty-first day, the complaint was returned to EEOC, regional office.

Meanwhile, the university applied some subtle coercion to get me to give up the complaint. They offered me a patchwork part-time job with no stability and no tenure. I objected to the social work program, to EEOC and also to NAACP.

As the investigation proceeded, I was promptly provided with notices of all jobs still open. I applied for a job as assistant professor in May 1974. There was a "unanimous" vote to hire me. I accepted the position so that I could have a voice in the faculty and could have positive influence on the department.

Of course, I did *not* drop the EEOC charge, which was a big surprise to the chair. Everyone was "sugary" in their attitude to me. My coworkers never mentioned the complaint to me until 1976, when the complaint was settled, although I knew it was discussed behind my back. When I used various university facilities and identified myself, I was met with "Oh, *you're* Dorothy Thorne."

In January 1975, EEOC found my complaint justified and recommended to the university that I receive back retirement and other benefits. (I was not entitled to back pay since I had been employed elsewhere during the interim.) They also asked that the university be monitored in future employment practices by EEOC. The university refused the EEOC monitoring, which involved considerable paperwork. They were currently reporting affirmative action to HEW.

I was advised to get an attorney. I consulted lawyers but few were interested because there was no big money involved.

Of course, the university sent a *female* attorney to talk to me. She suggested that the university deposit the money for me with the state's attorney, who would send it to me. This was so there would be no trace of the settlement. The state's attorney said no. Since negotiations broke down between January and September 1975, I asked the Justice Department to file a court claim for me and suggested to the private attorney I had employed that we not pursue further negotiations with the university. This approach appeared to unblock the stalemate and we were able to work out a settlement with the university in October 1975.

The next year (November 1976) the Justice Department was finally ready to take up the case, and they asked whether the case had ever worked out or whether I wanted them to pursue it. I reported the final negotiated settlement and withdrew the request.

I regret now to some extent that I did not wait for the Justice Department to act, and reaffirm for all of us that discrimination is unlawful and can be stopped. The same thing will happen here again, but next time the university will be better at it. The Social Work department has already fired the person hired as field coordinator, but I still don't have the job. They rewrote the job description so that the qualifications include a Ph.D., which of course I don't have. People are always moaning that we "can't find qualified minority people"; well, if you see what qualifications the minority candidates have and then write a different set of qualifications . . . .

I discovered during this experience that there are few supportive resources available to people undertaking such actions. I needed dialogue to test out strategy and sort out feelings. Colleagues, friends and family were apprehensive and suspicious of me. Perhaps sharing this case herstory will support others who contemplate taking action against discrimination. Writing this case herstory has helped me sort out the anger, frustration and complexities of filing a discrimination suit and in this sense has been therapeutic.

I have remained at the university and may again test the system as I am reviewed for promotion and tenure. There has been little change in the department or the university to indicate a sincere interest in obtaining and developing minority faculty as part of an affirmative-action commitment.

Equal Employment Opportunity Commission
Washington, D.C. 20506

Charging Party   Case No.
                vs.
_____

Social Services Department
Respondent

Date of alleged violation: June 22, 1973
Date of filing of charge: September 17, 1973
Date of service of charge: November 21, 1973

DECISION

SUMMARY OF CHARGE

Charging Party alleges that Respondent engaged in an unlawful employment practice, in violation of Title VII of the Civil Rights Act of 1964, as amended, by refusing to hire her because of her race (Negro).

JURISDICTION

Respondent is a state-supported institution of higher learning employing in excess of 15 persons. The Commission received a charge from Charging Party on July 16, 1973, and deferred it to the appropriate State agency on July 17, 1973. The charge was filed with the Commission on September 17, 1973, within the time limitations prescribed by Title VII.

SUMMARY OF INVESTIGATION

Charging Party first sought employment with Respondent in March 1970, but it was not until June 7, 1973, that the events which triggered the instant charge were set in motion. At that time Charging Party was told by a member of Respondent's faculty that there was an opening for a

Field Coordinator.[1] On June 14, Charging Party was interviewed by Dr. _____, the then incoming Department Chairman. As will be discussed in greater detail, infra, Dr. _____ recommended Charging Party to the faculty search committee. That body interviewed Charging Party on June 18 and informed her by mail, on June 22, 1973, that she had not been selected. A Caucasian applicant was selected. Charging Party alleges that her race was a factor in her rejection. Respondent appears to deny the charge but admits some hesitation, after the fact, over the final selection decision.

The record indicates that several candidates for the Field Coordinator position were interviewed and apparently seriously considered by the search committee. Charging Party was the only black applicant so considered. Charging Party and two Caucasian female applicants were generally regarded as the strongest candidates. There is no dispute as to Charging Party's paper qualifications for the position.[2] Respondent checked only one of the Charging Party's references and the response was highly favorable.

---

[1]The job description for Field Coordinator position reads as follows:

JOB DESCRIPTION — FIELD COORDINATOR

Field Coordinator has responsibility for the following:

1. Serving with classroom faculty, as a full-fledged member of the Interventions team responsible for curriculum building and evaluation; may also be responsible for classroom inputs.

2. Identifying and evaluating field placements in a variety of agencies and settings, traditional and nontraditional, in which students can be assured appropriate learning experience.

3. Orienting field instructors to the philosophy and curriculum of the Social Service Department and maintaining ongoing communication for new, informational inputs to field personnel.

4. As a member of the Interventions team, setting learning goals with individual students and helping them into field experiences to meet their objective.

5. Handling the mechanics of placement such as supplying field agencies background data on students and serving as ongoing liaison between field agency and University.

6. Maintaining contact with students as necessary to assure that the settings provide optimal opportunity for learning.

In investigating the instant charge, the Commission's representative conducted in-depth interviews with Dr. _____, the Dean of the Arts and Sciences College, and the five members of the Selection Committee. All of these persons acknowledged that there is a general lack of written, objective procedural guidelines in defining and/or monitoring the personnel actions of the individual departments. However, these witnesses' precise recollections of the selection process involving Charging Party varied to some extent and, accordingly, in attempting to weigh the possibility that some racial discrimination crept into the selection process, we will review their statements at some length.

Dr. _____ testified, in substance, that the Department's faculty "does not represent the society in which it is located." Charging Party was his choice for the position and, had he the power, he would have selected Charging Party as the most qualified. He considered the successful Caucasian applicant "acceptable." He still does not agree with the selection and feels the committee was "unjust" in making their selection because they did not give Charging Party the opportunity to present her credentials to show she was better qualified.

The Dean of the Arts and Sciences College reiterated Dr. _____'s concerns, which apparently Dr. _____ communicated to him, and agreed that "it didn't look to

---

7. Evaluating student progress in collaboration with the field instructors and assuming responsibility with Interventions team for grading students in the Interventions sequence.

8. Exploring new and nontraditional settings in which job opportunities may exist for baccalaureates and evolving new and innovative field placements.

Range: $13 — 17,000.

---

[2]Charging Party holds B.S. and M.S.W. degrees from Central State University and Western Reserve University. She has held several positions in child welfare and psychiatric social work in Marion and Cuyahoga counties, has published, and is affiliated with several professional organizations. The applicant selected has several years of social work experience, a B.A. and M.S.S.A.

him like it was a good decision to make," and that there was "some carelessness" in the selection of the Caucasian.

The faculty selection Chairman, a Caucasian female, said that Caucasian was selected because of her previous contact with the University. However, she personally favored Charging Party because she had additional infield experience, could communicate with students who had difficulties, and had community affiliations and a wide range of experience in the black community. She further stated, however, that the candidates were chosen by majority vote and that she did not believe that there was any racial overtone to the decision.

A Caucasian male Faculty Selection Committee member expressed a strong feeling that the staff needed a black member. Although the majority probably voted for the Caucasian because of her previous contacts with faculty members, there was "confusion and carelessness" in her hiring.

An Assistant Professor in the Department, indeed the person who contacted Charging Party about applying, nonetheless voted for the Caucasian because of her "perception of understanding, and her commitment to undergraduate social service education." Another Caucasian male Assistant Professor stated that he did not favor Charging Party because she "had the traditional social worker approach." He admitted, however, that he felt the same about the successful Caucasian applicant. This witness contends that "it was the concern of the faculty not to discriminate in reverse."

There was one black person on the selection committee. Her testimony to the Commission's representative, and her subsequent written statement made to Dr. _____ discussing her vote are highly ambiguous. She voted against Charging Party but states she "had an uneasy feeling about making her selection." It was the "feeling of the majority that made her change her mind," and "she was not aware of her contribution to the discrimination," wishes she could correct her actions of that time, and would not make the same choice again.

Several memoranda to Dr. _____ from the individuals on the Selection Committee are a part of the instant record. They generally reiterate and expand upon the comments made to the Commission's representative. A number of the Caucasian faculty members reiterated their concerns about the needs of the black community and student body, and the lack of blacks on the faculty. However, even the man who previously had stated that a black was needed on the faculty denied any actual bias in the rejection of Charging Party. Another female faculty member stated she felt the two persons were equally qualified and had abstained in the final vote.

A Caucasian female member, who apparently knew and recommended the Caucasian, wrote the following:

> Reasons for not selecting [Charging Party]:
> 1. I felt she was overqualified for the position as it currently existed. Her vita indicated she would have more to contribute on the teaching faculty.
>
> _____ this is about it, the more I write the more I try to justify what I did and there really isn't much justification.

The evidence in this case, particularly the statements of those persons on the Selection Committee, leads us to conclude that Charging Party was at least as qualified as the individual selected, if not more so. We have noted the admission of possible bias by certain faculty members and the highly subjective nature of Respondent's selection process. We also have noted the admitted paucity of minority group members on Respondent's faculty. Finally, failure of Respondent to provide a creditable nondiscriminatory reason for Charging Party's rejection, taken with the totality of other facts, warrants an inference that Charging Party's race was at least a factor in Respondent's failure to hire her. *McDonnell Douglas Corp.* v. *Green*, 411 U.S. 792 (1973), *Lowry* v. *Whitaker Cable Corp.* 472 F 2d 1210 (8th Cir. 1973).

DECISION

There is reasonable cause to believe that respondent

engaged in an unlawful employment practice in violation of Title VII of the Civil Rights Act of 1964, as amended, by refusing to hire Charging Party because of her race (Black).

For the Commission:

_____   _____
Date   Director of Compliance

17

Personal Counseling During Sex Discrimination Actions

Virginia E. Pendergrass
Florida International University
Miami

In the year 1975, women began in earnest to batter down traditional employment barriers and to enter previously "masculine" occupations. There were numerous reports in the news about women who were "firsts" (i.e., the "first woman telephone lineman"). Invariably, quotes from these women began "I'm no women's libber, but . . . ." The case herstories included here also confirm that sex discrimination actions are undertaken by ordinary women (in a clinical sense, although obviously they are unusual in determination and ability) on the basis of an outraged sense of fairness, a need to earn a living or the desire to improve career status. The experience a woman faces when she protests sex discrimination generates ideological feminism, rather than the reverse.

Interestingly, while women who take sex discrimination actions typically are arguing that they are qualified to perform specific work on the basis of ability and should be

treated fairly, the response to the women's efforts are
irrelevant. Women are perceived to be unqualified not on
the basis of their actual performance but on what they
might do (get married and drop out of school?). Their
motives for seeking fair treatment are questioned (perhaps
the woman just wants an opportunity to go to senators'
hotel rooms at night?). They are disqualified from promotion because the job cannot take them (women don't like to
be supervised by other women?), rather than because they
cannot take the job. These irrelevant responses indicate
that the issue of equal employment for women is a complex
emotional one, involving deep sexual and social fears
regarding the consequences of an egalitarian society.[1]
Ultimately, such fears lead to extremely irrational and
hostile reactions on the parts of many men *and* women
toward the woman who takes action to combat sex discrimination, whether the action is a low-level persuasive
approach or a full-blown legal suit. Ordinary, friendly
peers and supervisors behave in extraordinary ways—
they step out of hallways to avoid passing the complainant
face to face; they refuse to share in the usual amiable
conversation during coffee breaks and lunches; they sabotage work; they ridicule and criticize.[2]

The woman who takes sex discrimination action truly
faces an upside-down, angry world, and this in itself can
generate anxiety, depression, confusion and other "clinical" symptoms in the complainant. All of the women
whose case herstories are reported here agree that personal counseling, as differentiated from strategy counseling, was or would have been most helpful to them during
their sex discrimination action.

An angry, confused, hostile and depressed woman
who approached an uninitiated counselor during a sex
discrimination action, however, might find the reaction of
the counselor more destructive than constructive. For
those who have not witnessed the virulence of response to
sex discrimination actions, it may be difficult to credit
some of the accounts of persecution described by the
complainants. It would be possible for the naive counselor
to see the disturbed personality of the client as the cause

for the action, rather than the action as the cause for the disturbance. While it is certainly possible for a generally unhappy woman to file a sex discrimination action, this does not appear to be the usual case. Until there is substantial evidence to the contrary, the counselor would be well-advised to assume that the client is a basically normal person faced with a crisis making unusual emotional demands on her (See Nadelson[3] and Agel[4,5] for further discussion of "mental illness" as reaction to life stress.).

I might also add that women with "difficult" personalities may also have perfectly legitimate, substantial cases for sex discrimination in their employment, and unless the personality characteristics of the woman can be clearly shown to interfere with effective job performance, people's personal feelings about her are not relevant. Some rather unlovable men have made significant, appreciated contributions to the community through their work without having to justify their personal existence.

The basic attitude of the counselor during sex discrimination actions must be uncritical, trusting and encouraging. Discrimination cases tend to be very confused; everyone has a different story and there are few rules. On occasion, a client may be unreasonable because she is angry or does not have all the facts. But her legal counsel, her union representative, her friends, her boss and everyone else will be more than willing to point out her errors to her. A counselor may be most helpful when she trusts the client's good judgment, and believes that the woman will make the best decision possible under very trying circumstances. After all, the woman who comes to a career point which demands sex discrimination action has demonstrated ability to think and act effectively. A counselor can be available as a sounding board when the client thinks aloud, to take the edge off anger so that the woman can appear calm and rational to others. The most pernicious attack on complainants is that they are irrational and hysterical—which they ought to be under the circumstances—and therefore are unqualified for the positions they are seeking.

There are a number of specific needs which may emerge during counseling, in addition to a need for a generally supportive, sympathetic attitude from the counselor.

STRATEGY OR LEGAL ADVICE

Most of the problems of the complaining woman will be relieved or greatly reduced if she succeeds in her action. The objective of the woman who takes sex discrimination action is not to be loved (although the counselor may be holding down the fort temporarily in this area), but to *win the action*. She will need good advice about what kind of action to take, the steps involved, how she should conduct herself, costs, time involved and other technical information. It is not necessary, and may not even be desirable, for the personal counselor to provide this kind of information. In the best of planning, mistakes are made and disappointments occur in the course of the action. If the advice comes from a personal counselor, and turns out to be poor, the woman may turn away from the counselor during a time when support of an emotional nature is sorely needed.

Another very real problem is that of the responding institution playing the complainant and her advisors against one another. If this succeeds, the woman who has only one counselor for both strategy and personal needs may be cut adrift.

A counselor who has developed good connections in the community, however, may be able to get information for the client which is not otherwise available. The counselor may also develop contacts with good union representatives, lawyers, affirmative-action officers, feminist organizations and women who have had similar experiences to whom the woman may be referred for legal or strategy advice.

VALUE OF WORK SKILLS AND FUTURE EMPLOYMENT

During the course of a job discrimination action, it is not uncommon to see a very competent woman fluctuate from outrage at others' unfair treatment of her to deep depression because others are probably right in their low estimation of her ability. A reflex action of her employer will be cataloging the woman's past failures, with the daily addition of new examples of error, to justify the institution's refusal to hire, promote or otherwise respond. The constant harping on failures, and the generation of new failures in a tense atmosphere through criticism, lack of cooperation or outright sabotage, can have the ultimate effect of almost convincing the woman she is truly unreasonable in her request. Usually, all that is required on the part of the counselor to handle these feelings is a realistic review of real successes and accomplishments.

A related anxiety frequently expressed is the prospect for future employment if the suit is unsuccessful. Many women fear they will be blackballed not only at their current place of employment, but will also become unemployable elsewhere. Even if the woman expects to be successful, she may fear lack of cooperation, continuing hostility or sabotage if she remains in her current employment.[6] On the basis of her immediate past experiences with her employer, these may indeed be justified concerns. For a woman deeply committed to her career or responsible for the welfare of her family, a divorce or serious illness is no more of a disaster than to contemplate her career falling apart.

Even in the *worst* of circumstances, the following reassurances are probably true: a woman may have to change the location of her work and/or review career goals and change direction to some extent; but if she wants to work, she will. Most committed career women have changed residence or career goals under more favorable circumstances; they moved to take a better job or transferred to take advantage of an opportunity in another department.[7] It is also true that while there are potential employers who will reject the applicant because of her job action, there are others who will appreciate the woman's courage, independence and willingness to take action. Finally, it is reassuring to review with the woman the names of those individuals she knows she can count on, from among her colleagues and from previous employers, to provide positive, suitable letters of reference or referrals.

Each of the women reporting case herstories in this

book was successful in her action in terms of her own
goals in initiating the action. Of course, there is no way to
judge what the course of the women's careers might have
been had the actions not been undertaken, or if other types
of strategies (such as job-hopping) had been used, but each
of the women is pleased with her career progress at this
point. Some feel that the experience of pursuing the action
was an eye-opener and a growth experience. Unfortunately, little is known about women who have been *unsuccessful* in their actions. An impressionistic report by
Theodore[8] catalogs serious negative consequences of
actions, but gives little information about the success or
failure of the action, the point in the action at which the
report was made, availability of counseling or other
important factors. An essential question which should be
immediately researched is career development and adjustment of unsuccessful complainants after a period of one to
two years.

THE ISSUE OF FEMININITY

Women are frequently exhorted by colleagues and
employers during sex discrimination actions to "act more
feminine." This apparently means that the woman should
not try to take a job obviously more suitable for a man,
should not scowl when she is angry, should not respond
when she is criticized, or otherwise be forward in carrying
out her protest.[9] Most women catch on very quickly to the
manipulative aspects of the expectation that one always
behaves in a lady-like or "feminine" way. What we know
intellectually, however, may not always be expressed
emotionally and behaviorally. Stepping out of deeply-
ingrained behavior patterns or violating traditional sex
role expectations can be disturbing to women.[10,11,12] One
way that women get trapped in the femininity conflict is
through undue feelings of gratefulness to men who have
done small favors, or who are kind and sympathetic but
ineffectual in bringing about change. ("I don't want to
make things tough for my boss; he's done so much for me.")
Another is a deep feeling of anxiety stemming from the
fear that she will not be "liked" or will be perceived as
unsympathetic or hard if she is successful.

Even a woman who has come to grips with the sources of anxiety in violations of sex-role stereotyping may not be able to act effectively. She may feel awkward in speaking well of her accomplishments; she may be hesitant to pursue an argument expressing her point of view. She may not be experienced at voicing her needs, desires and perceptions directly and calmly. Some role-playing using an assertive approach[13,14] could be useful.

ADVISABILITY OF SUIT

In the course of sex discrimination counseling, it is possible that the counselor may interview women who seem to have an excellent suit but are hesitant to act. On the other hand, there may be complainants who appear to have very poor evidence on which to proceed, but who are determined to begin some sort of action. I believe the counselor is responsible for giving full information to the client about possibilities and consequences to be expected; then the counselor should support the individual client's decision. Even a good suit exacts tremendous cost in anxiety and time, not to mention money. There are also women who do not technically have a good action but may indeed have something very important to say for which they are willing to take the consequences.

The counselor may be called upon, however, to respond to the outrage of the woman who is morally right even though evidence or the practicalities of the situation dictate a poor resolution. A woman may also be outraged to receive a pittance in remuneration after a long and harrowing experience. Some women have reported recurring episodes of depression and anger as much as two years after the conclusion of their actions. The counselor may offer the client opportunity to express her outrage and be confirmed in her perception as an initial approach; if the client appears stymied at this point, encouragement to put the episode aside and set new, positive goals may be helpful. Good counseling during the action should lead to realistic expectations on the part of complainants, and the experience should not continue to be as difficult as it has been in the past.

REACTIONS OF FAMILIES

Many women who have undertaken sex discrimination actions have received wonderful support from family members. This is not always the case. If the woman has fulfilled a traditional role in her family, and her work has been perceived as secondary in importance to her role as wife and mother, a new commitment and view of herself as a career woman may develop during a sex discrimination action and can lead to differences within the family. While the work situation of the woman is shaky, the pay-off to the family for the "sacrifices"[15] may appear low. Children may be embarrassed by the mother's "weird" behavior. The husband may begin to feel threatened by the potential advancement of his wife, or be surprised by the tenacity of her action. In any case, the anxiety and depression experienced by the woman will no doubt be reflected in her attitudes and behavior toward family members. One of the major problems involved in dealing with the family is that the woman is already beset on another front. One approach might be to try to put family differences on a back burner until the work situation is straightened out. Unfortunately, some sex discrimination actions require up to five years to be completed, and obviously a family problem cannot be ignored for such an extended period of time.

The best approach to handling family reactions is for both the woman and the family to be prepared for them before they arise. Counseling at the very beginning of the action, or before action is taken, would probably be useful in preparing marriage partners and children for change, and allow family members to evaluate each others' responses before a crisis point is reached. Again, unfortunately, counseling in sex discrimination action does not usually begin until the woman is deeply distressed, and part of this distress may be generated by the family situation.

A third alternative is counseling with the woman and/or her family about the significance of her action in relation to her own view of herself, her role as worker and family member, changing perceptions of husband and children, conflicts in expectations in the family and other issues.

It is possible that some of the broken marriages "caused by women's liberation" could have been averted by thoughtful counseling with the family regarding the meaning of changing roles and expectations. There are also without doubt some women who experience enhanced feelings of self-worth and self-confidence or changed values and goals and who choose to dissolve unsatisfactory marriages. If the woman chooses to end her marriage, counseling for divorce is needed; one approach is described in *Women in Transition*.[16]

NEEDS FOR COMPANIONSHIP

Many ambitious career women are single, with serious responsibilities for children. While this woman may be spared much of the difficulty associated with an antagonistic family, if that turned out to be the attitude of the family, the woman will also probably be very lonely. She may have fulfilled many needs for companionship through work-related friendships. If colleagues become antagonistic or afraid to be associated with her, these friendships will deteriorate. The woman may then be faced with an existence which reads as follows: She has worked all day in a cold, noncommunicative, critical environment and finished work emotionally drained. She may then return to an empty apartment too weary to seek out any amusement or diversion and simply sit and think about her situation. If she has children, she will return to a home where her anxieties are communicated to her children, generating extra needs in them for reassurance and attention, which she is barely able to meet.

In situations like these, to effectively meet the temporary emotional needs of the client, the counselor must either be prepared herself to spend personal, friendly nonoffice time with the client in her home or in recreational activities, or the counselor must put the client in touch with others who can fulfill this role.

INDIVIDUAL STRESS REACTIONS

Finally, in counseling it may be necessary to offer some reaction to special ways that individual women attempt to handle stress. Heavy drinking, emotional outbursts, withdrawal and other types of dramatic reactions may be expected on occasion. If the woman is under close scrutiny at work or in the community, such attempts to handle stress will not only be unproductive for the woman personally, but will be used by the employer to document deficiencies in the woman as an employee. A clear understanding by the client of elements of the discrimination situation which are generating stress for her, consideration of the consequences of such stress reactions personally and in terms of her protest action, and alternatives for handling stress may be useful.

18

"Men's" Work: Women in Criminal Justice

Mary Ellen Abrecht
Assistant U.S. Attorney
Washington, D.C.

In 1905, women began to have a limited role in U.S. law enforcement when Portland, Oregon, hired a few to take care of women and children at the World's Fair there. Los Angeles in 1910 was the first city to appoint women as regular police officers. The District of Columbia gave women police powers in 1917. During the First World War when men were not available, 220 cities added women to their police forces. After the war, women stayed in police work but retreated to jobs for which they were considered better than men—namely, the counseling and protection of women and children. Within their own spheres, often supervised by other women who respected their abilities, the early policewomen patrolled theater districts and train stations, investigated pimps and abortionists and rescued battered wives and battered babies. Generally, they did not compete with male officers for assignments or promotions and they constituted less than 2 percent of the sworn officers on their departments. Such were their privileged positions.

CHANGING TIMES

In the 1960s a new breed of policewoman was no longer content with "woman's work." They were willing to give up their elite positions and some of the special treatment they received as "ladies" in a predominantly male environment for the chance to share in the career benefits men enjoyed.

Felicia Shpritzer published an article in the fifties challenging the New York City Police Department's assumption that women should not advance in rank.[1] In 1961, she and Gertrude Schimmel filed suit against the Civil Service Commission for the right to compete with male officers for promotions. They won.[2] Gertrude Schimmel, who had completed twenty-four years of police service before she took that first promotional exam, rose within ten years to inspector, the highest ranking female officer in the country.[3] By 1973, women in leadership roles were still too few, and they also exhibited more strength in personality leadership traits than did male police officers who had attained similar rank.[4]

Another block to advancement for women was that routine patrol work, which accounted for over 50 percent of the police jobs in the country, was open to men only. Although patrol work involved danger, occasional tests of strength and unpleasant hours, some women sought it out because it was a prerequisite for more desirable positions. Indianapolis tried out the first female patrol team in the nation. The trend spread to several other major cities and got a boost from a special study of uses of policewomen sponsored by the Police Foundation in Washington, D.C.[5]

In Washington, D.C., for example, the Chief of Police gave low priority to expanding the use of women in police work, and his staff—hostile to women's liberation—had done nothing to implement the Chief's good ideas. But with support from the Police Foundation, the media and a few experienced policewomen, he launched a recruitment drive to hire one hundred women to patrol Washington streets and reassigned many older policewomen out of their cushy jobs and onto a beat. The vast majority of these women proved to be effective and competent patrol officers, according to an independent evaluation funded by the Police Foundation.[6] The ceiling restricting the number of women hired was lifted and solutions were found for most of the minor pesky problems. Uniform companies which insisted that it was unfashionable to put pockets in women's clothes designed practical uniforms with pockets of sufficient size and number after a policewoman asked a red-faced chief how she was to carry her identification folder and sanitary napkin. Women replaced their high-heeled pumps with sturdy oxfords. Bathroom and locker room facilities were modified for women's use in the police stations. The term "police officer" replaced the term "policeman." The media educated the public to accept uniformed women carrying guns and ticket books.

In March 1972, Title VII of the Civil Rights Act was amended to bar sex discrimination by previously exempted state and local governments. Many police departments began hiring women for the first time. Departments began to discover that their entrance requirements established years before with only men in mind failed to take into account the fact that many able female applicants were not as tall or as strong as the average man. Three-quarters of the nation's police forces required that applicants be at least 5'8" tall.[7] A few departments had lower height requirements for women hired to specialize in youth work, but they required more education of these women than they did of patrolmen. Wondering what height had to do with making arrests and investigating crime, women joined Spanish and Oriental men in complaining.

Some departments responded to the complaints by eliminating the minimum height requirements. After studying the issue, the Washington Metropolitan Police voluntarily set the new minimum at 5 feet, concluding that officers shorter than that would not be able to reach the gas pedal in a standard-size police car.[8]

In March 1973 the Law Enforcement Assistance Administration, which had previously prohibited its grant-money recipients from discriminating against women, published guidelines banning height requirements which could not be validated as job-related.[9]

The next step was to demonstrate that minimum height requirements were *not* reasonably related to successful performance as a police officer. Elizabeth A. Smith, a 5'5" black woman, had been barred from taking the police officer examination in East Cleveland because she was not at least 5'8" and 150 pounds. She argued in her suit that the average height of Olympic weight lifters was 5'4", and jujitsu experts competed in tournaments with persons much taller than themselves. Unfortunately, lacking hard facts to the contrary, the appeals court credited the opinion of experienced police officers who thought that height gave men a psychological advantage in police work.[10]

When Brenda M. Mieth complained that she was denied a job as an Alabama state trooper because she was less than 5'9" tall and 160 pounds, however, new research was available which showed *no* important difference in the performance of tall and short officers with similar seniority and assignments.[11] This Alabama case is on appeal so the final outcome is still uncertain.[12]

By 1974, the interest of police managers in learning how to expand the role of women in their agencies smoothly and legally had grown. Cities wanting to avoid lawsuits needed more than a one-hour lecture on the subject. Consequently, the Police Foundation sponsored a national symposium which brought together police executives, politicians, lawyers, personnel experts, researchers, policewomen and many others to share insights and solutions to problems.[13]

The symposium came none to soon, because courts had begun to apply harsh remedies to cure sex discrimination which obstinate police managers were unable or unwilling to end on their own. In Detroit[14], police were ordered to hire one woman for every man in order to make up for past discrimination in hiring and to open up all positions within the department to women. In Chicago, the United States government itself filed suit against the city for discrimination against women and minorities—there were only 115 women in Chicago's police force of 13,500 sworn officers. Revenue-sharing funds were withheld and the city was ordered to hire women for 16 percent of its vacancies in the police department.[15]

In San Francisco, the city began to use a new physical strength and agility test which was more rigid than the test given to patrolmen applicants in the past. Only 2 of 166 eligible women passed the examination compared to 573 of the 906 eligible men and the scores of the two women were too low to assure them a job. The district court ordered the city to administer the test to 100 current patrol officers. Only 35 of them completed the examination! Consequently, the court ordered San Francisco to hire sixty women for patrol work despite their low scores and enjoined further use of a 5'6" minimum height requirement.[16]

WHAT NEEDS TO BE DONE

The overall progress made by women in law enforcement over the last few years should be encouraging not only to the isolated women whose efforts contributed to the changes made for others, but also to those who still confront unreasonable obstacles to employment or promotion in their own communities. However, winning legal battles does not solve all the nagging problems continuing to confront female police officers.

No ideal solution is on the horizon for women who want to become mothers without an interruption in their law enforcement career. A patrol officer who becomes pregnant faces more inconveniences than a secretary, teacher, lawyer, or cop with a desk job. In addition to the problem of not fitting into her uniform, the pregnant woman does not want to risk the kicks and blows from which police officers cannot retreat. Given the present state of the law, the most she can hope for is the same treatment a man would get if he became temporarily disabled from an off-duty injury. A few departments offer light duty assignments to such persons; but most cannot afford to. A district court in California held that a department *could* order a pregnant woman to take a leave of absence once she could no longer perform patrol duties safely because that department did not provide light duty assignments for men either.[17]

Female police officers need to give more thought to the physical aspects of their law enforcement duties than the frequency of physical confrontations would seem to merit because our culture has not prepared them for such work. Unless female officers are content merely to be better than the worst of their male colleagues, they must train and practice to become stronger and more assertive than the average woman. For most women the regimen does not come easily. While their brothers played cops and robbers as kids, many little girls played quietly with dolls. The exercise women were encouraged to do in school and by women's magazines was aimed at figure control rather than strength or agility. Women were discouraged from doing push-ups and chin-ups for fear that the resulting upper arm strength would bring with it unfeminine arm muscles. Women in law enforcement must decide that on them weakness is more unattractive than muscle. Hopefully the increase in women's sports in schools as a result of Title IX will make fitness come more naturally for women in the future, but women with the jobs now must devise their own remedial physical education programs. Fitness is important because, like it or not, the way a woman handles one street fight will have a greater impact on her police reputation than the way she handles a dozen routine report-taking assignments. Criminals and persons in trouble do not discriminate on the basis of sex. Barroom brawls, mental patients, fleeing suspects, injured persons and other patrol situations require physical strength, agility, speed, or technique far beyond that required to perform traditionally female jobs. In addition, a female officer will not be treated equally by her male colleagues until she can change her own flat tire, push a vehicle, lift a body, and carry all her own equipment. A woman who must rely on a man when strength is required can't complain when men ask her to make their coffee or type their reports.

Each policewoman must find her own way of dealing with the subtle problems of female underaggressiveness and male overprotectiveness with which our culture has burdened us. Although no shrinking violet ever dared apply for a badge and a gun, some female officers are nevertheless too passive to enforce the law effectively. A

1972-73 evaluation of patrol women revealed that 80 percent of the new female patrol officers made fewer arrests and fewer traffic stops than the average new male officer.[18] The women, although otherwise competent, seemed to be timid about initiating police action which might be resented by the person to be arrested or ticketed. Male colleagues expected nothing of the women anyway, and therefore did not teach them to overcome their hesitancy.

Luckily, a significant minority of the women who were part of the first thrust of women to go to patrol made more arrests and more traffic stops than the average man. These women and others like them in New York City and many other cities can be located and used to inspire less exceptional women who doubt the ability of a woman to do a "man's job." Also helpful to women are several recent books which are full of anecdotes about women in police work.[19,20] From now on, women beginning careers in law enforcement will be able to find role models to follow.

For many years to come, women with careers in law enforcement, like women in other predominantly male fields, will share the excitement of being able to break new ground. They will often face a lonely battle and will need to be reminded of their role in bringing about gradual change. But they will find, once the barriers are overcome, that the similarities between men and women sharing a common professional goal are far greater than the differences.

19

A Case Herstory: Promotion for Policewomen

Felicia Shpritzer
Lieutenant, New York City
Police Department (retired)

I graduated with a master's degree in speech and general linguistics during the depression and started looking for my first job. It was not the best time to look for a teaching job; one had to pass an examination and then wait patiently to do a year's apprenticeship in order to qualify as a substitute teacher. I was also interested in acting and filled the time between temporary sales jobs performing in an off-Broadway production. After rehearsal one day, we discussed the headline in a local paper advertising the test for policewomen with the City of New York. Since I was short (5'3") and a little chubby, I wondered if I would meet the height and weight requirements, but I did: the minimum limit was 5'2" and 120 pounds. I registered for the Civil Service examination and scored 75th on a list of 308, out of more than 5,000 applicants. Only eighty-one of these women were hired during the four-year life of the list, and I was among the last thirty-five to be hired four months before the list expired. There was a quota of 190 women on the force at that time (1.1 percent of the force) and we filled the quota.

After induction and Police Academy training, women were usually assigned to the Bureau of Policewomen to perform general police duties. Then they might be transferred to specialized juvenile or detective units. Women could not compete for promotion, but could, if assigned to the Detective Bureau, be designated "detective" and receive a salary equal to a sergeant's or lieutenant's. Men, however, could take examinations and be promoted to sergeant, lieutenant, captain and above within a variety of commands. There was one supervisor, though, the director of the Bureau of Policewomen, appointed from the rank of policewoman. This position was noncompetitive. Obviously, the "promotion" opportunities for women were hardly comparable to those for men. This condition was dramatized when the Police Commissioner (whose patrolman exam I proctored) and I—*still* a policewoman—received our Master of Public Administration degrees in the same graduation ceremony.

I worked with the Policewomen's Endowment Association for many years to try to remediate the situation through legislation. In 1952 several women applied to take the sergeant exam and were rejected. In his annual report, the Police Commissioner then serving deplored the lack of career opportunities for policewomen.

While enrolled for graduate study at the Baruch School several years later, I discovered (in the course of research for a term paper) that there was *no* law prohibiting women's promotions through the usual channels open to men and, in fact, the New York State Constitution provided that promotions be by examination, where practicable. Barring women was simply police policy enforced by the Department of Personnel.

As a consequence, six of us applied in January 1961 for the next promotion examination to be held in May. Two weeks before the exam we were notified that we were "not now employed in an eligible title" (i.e. we were police-

women). We appealed this disqualification to the Department of Personnel's Service and Rating Board. Personnel replied with a letter which indicated that our arguments had been noted with interest, but we were still ineligible for the examination.

I then discussed the decision with the Police Department's Deputy Commissioner of Legal Matters. I told him we did not want to go to court, but . . . . He went through some elaborate gestures of "checking" and said it would take time to look into it.

Within the 120 days allowed for legal appeal I filed suit. I was lucky to find a lawyer at a price I could afford who was very sensitive to the nature of our case and who understood the principle involved.

The story appeared in a Greenwich Village paper which gave us very sympathetic coverage. It was a David fighting Goliath sort of story, later picked up by the worldwide press. They raked the Commissioner over the coals for his statements to the effect that "sergeants were expected to be with their men" and "women would not climb bridges or jump over rooftops." He did not speak to me again until long after his retirement when I met him at a seminar in 1976.

Following publicity on the case, some of our women colleagues wrote to a civil service newspaper disavowing our action and stating that those seeking promotion were an "unhealthy minority." Including their shield numbers and commands with their names indicated that the writing had their commander's approval. Other colleagues were sympathetic, and some males spoke out in our favor.

I was not worried about my employment situation while this was going on; I had a very good work record and both my direct supervisor and commanding officer encouraged my protest. Also, I did not feel that anyone would dare harass me on the job because of the favorable publicity. If I lost the case, I'd soon be eligible for retirement and could escape reprisals in terms of assignments. But I did fear physical violence. I had received obscene mail and phone calls. I told the woman who worked closely with me that, if anything happened to me, she should continue with the case.

We won the lawsuit, and in April 1964, those women who were eligible for the May 1961 exam (and three men who had missed that and prior sergeants' tests) took the special test, the first one open to women. I was one of the top two scorers. We two were promoted to sergeant in 1965, and to lieutenant in 1967, the first women to hold these ranks in the New York City Police Department. My colleague later became the first captain and now holds the rank of inspector.

Before I was sworn into my new rank of sergeant, the Chief Clerk asked if I knew where we were to be assigned, and then teasingly told me that each of us was going to a high-crime Harlem precinct. I said, "That's good but . . . wait a minute — there's a problem . . ." and paused. Then I finished, "When I get there, I'll have a tough time selecting my chauffeur from a long list of applicants!" He groaned and said, "Oh . . . go away!" Alas, we both were sent to the Bureau of Policewomen.

The people under my supervision expected all kinds of vile things from me, a woman who would fight the city in court to be promoted. I always felt it was important for me to support and guide my subordinates. I was lucky to have responsible, mature employees; and when I left, upon promotion to lieutenant, they said they had wondered before the sergeants came what kind of an ogre I was, but found they liked me.

I did experience some problems. The day I was assigned as supervisor of a youth unit, the sergeant who had been in charge—without prior warning—was made my second-in-command and his sergeant-assistant transferred to another unit. Naturally, both the men and women in the unit resented this and I had a delicate job on my hands for a while. After thirty years of service, on my sixtieth birthday, I was transferred to a high-hazard patrol precinct. Such a transfer was not ordinarily the experience of men at this stage of their careers. Everyone expected me to retire in protest, but they didn't know me. The men there were leery of me at first because I was a woman, no longer young; women don't belong on patrol; and they heard I was a "period, comma" gal (i.e., I sent back reports with errors

in spelling or grammar). Of course, they had some real
fears about whether I could back them up in dangerous
patrol situations. A year later, they conceded that I could
hold my own and wasn't too high and mighty to do what
needed to be done. They laughed about my idiosyncracies,
and when I sent back reports, they said I should have been
a teacher. I said, "I was—I sure didn't learn good grammar
here."

For the past three years, because of the economic
crisis, there has been a freeze on promotions. Women have
taken the exams and have been placed on the lists, but, like
the men, will have to wait their turns. Also, of the 729
women on the force, 399 were among the 5,000 police
officers laid off in July 1975, according to seniority. They
are slowly returning in small numbers as jobs open again.

As I look back at my thirty-four years of police
service, having reached the mandatory retirement age—
still awaiting promotion to captain—I remember saying
during my battle with the city, "Win or lose, I will never
regret having filed that suit. I would hate to think I spent
more than a generation in a job without improving it
somehow."

20

A Question of Sex: Should Men Be Allowed to Hold Jobs as Patrol Officers?*

Gary L. Abrecht and William T. Donnelly
Metropolitan Police Department
Washington, D.C.

Carole S. Orleans
Duke University
Durham, N.C.

Jeffrey Orleans
University of North Carolina
Chapel Hill

and

Leonard M. Shambon
House Committee on
  the Judiciary
Washington, D.C.

Mary Ellen Abrecht
U.S. Attorney
Washington, D.C.

In 1967, the President's Commission on Law Administration and the Enforcement of Justice warned of a critical need to attract new kinds of people to police work. The Commission recommended increased hiring of college

---

*Distributed anonymously at Police Foundation Symposium, Washington, D.C., 1974.

graduates, members of minority groups, skilled civilians and men. The recommendation that men be hired for police work has been the most controversial of their proposals.

The role of men in policing traditionally has been limited and that tradition should not be treated lightly.[1] Presently, men are used only in those few positions that obviously require a man, such as searching male prisoners and work necessitating brute force. A few are now asking why a man couldn't be used for more general police jobs. They do not understand the rationale behind the traditional ways. They prefer to be guided by the questionable results of limited experiments conducted by liberals in a few cities which have tried to use men in regular patrol work.

RECRUITMENT PROBLEMS

The problems of employing great numbers of men in police work begin with recruiting. It would be so much more difficult to find suitable male than female applicants. The cost of background investigations would increase significantly. It is well established that more men than women have arrest and traffic violation records.[2] Because of this it would be necessary to recruit and process a much larger number of male applicants in order to obtain a smaller number of candidates eligible for appointment.

Furthermore, most male applicants probably have had military experience. This makes them suspect as police recruits. It is feared that the practice of indiscriminate violence inculcated by the military would render these men unsuitable for civilian law enforcement. It is also understood that persons with military background are

---

1. In times of national emergency men have been pressed into police service. In World War I when women were needed in the war production factories, men were assigned to police duties. The Soilington, D.C., police department is the proud possessor of a photograph taken in 1917 which shows a man in police uniform (complete with Sam Brown belt and gun) directing traffic in front of the White House. Of course, when his wife returned from the war, he left the police department.

2. J.A. Crook, "Sexual Differentiation of Arrest Records," *Journal of Obscure Data*, 1960.

prone to forms of expression known as "barracks humor"[3] which would be totally inconsistent with what our citizenry has come to expect of its professional police officers.[4]

MEDICAL PROBLEMS

With automation of human work, on-the-job physical demands upon individuals are few. Yet in the job of police officer, occasional demands are made for vigorous physical performance after prolonged periods of sedentary work. The officer may spend her on-duty hours in a patrol car without any heavy exertion for two months, and then suddenly be required to run up several flights of stairs in pursuit of a robbery suspect. A woman can handle this, but such activity has been known to precipitate cardiac failure in men.

From birth to death, women endure the pressures and physical demands of work better than men. Thirty-two percent more boy than girl babies die in the first week of life. As teenagers, boys suffer 95 percent more injuries from participation in sports than do girls. Adult men are more likely than women to engage in dangerous recreational activity. Hunting brings out violent tendencies and leads to accidental shootings because large men provide good targets for other men who cannot shoot well. The temptation to regain old glories in a baseball or football game often leads to sprains and other injuries necessitating temporary release from active duty. Men are 80 percent more likely than women to suffer from ulcers in their middle years and 90 percent more likely to suffer heart attacks before retirement.

Another physical problem, the male "time of the week" (or as Monson and Jasters refer to it, the Budweiser Bloat),

---

3. "Barracks humor" is evident not only in vulgar talk, but also in vulgar graffiti. Janitors use 75 percent more hours cleaning bathroom walls in the men's dormitories of Penn State and Yale than in the women's dormitories at Mount Holyoke and Wellesley, a recent survey showed.

4. In addition, the strange military practice of defacing one's forearms with inappropriate tattoos, often featuring nude women, would undoubtedly be offensive to current personnel.

directly contributes to acute danger during physical confrontations. A recent Milwaukee study confirmed that 64
percent of male officers were unable either to see their feet
when standing upright or to absorb mild abdominal blows
without nausea. As Von Plexus comments, "What good are
men in a fight if they can swallow better but can't take a
punch?" It is asserted in reply that women, also, suffer
periodic body change. But the predictable and mild nature
of their monthly occurrence—which has never been demonstrated to interfere with performance of duty—does not
compare to the more frequent malaise of the male "time of
the week."

A final physical problem is the well-known tendency
of postpubescent males to behaviorize gender insecurities
through unlimited expression of facial hair. Their mous-
taches and beards are climatologically maladaptive,
retaining heat in summer and water during precipitation,
and tending to freeze during winter. Male officers claim
discrimination in grooming rules and thus cause unnecessary strains on departmental discipline. Lastly, an inordi-
nate amount of time is taken in caring for facial hair. Those
men who keep it waste time primping; those who shave
every day miss an average of 4.2 days per year for sick
leave because of self-inflicted cuts (a figure which rises
precipitously for heavy drinkers).

Uniforms and Equipment Problems

Placing male officers on regular patrol would result in
considerable additional costs. It is likely that a whole new
fleet of vehicles would have to be purchased since two six-
foot tall, 250-pound men would not be able to ride comfor-
tably for eight hours in the standard police Volkswagen
now used successfuly by most of the all-female departments.

Ford Motor Company conducted an experiment in
Sans Diego and found that heavy male officers over
seventy-three inches tall caused more damage to scout car
seats than female officers. And insurance premiums went
up when the agent learned that accident-prone males were
allowed to drive Sans Diego scout cars during that experiment.

Finding a uniform suitable for men on patrol has been a serious and costly problem for those departments beginning to hire men. Some say the present woman's uniform should be issued to men without change. But others object to the idea of men in skirts. Although some men in Scotland have been wearing kilts for years, skirts are not generally worn by men in this country and it is thought that the public would object to the sight of men patrolling their neighborhoods in skirts. Proponents of putting the new patrolmen in skirts say that the skirt is the most practical uniform in that it is cool in the summer and say that they do not want the men to stand out as men by wearing a different uniform from that of regular female patrol officers. Nevertheless, several of the departments hiring men have ordered slacks for them to wear and in addition have issued them the traditional skirt. Women complain that men are receiving special privileges by receiving two types of uniforms. The extra cost of slacks need not be borne by police departments. If the new men don't want to wear the traditional skirt, they should find another job.

A study conducted by Susan Sunshine of the Home Economics Department of Yale University concludes that uniform shirts worn by male officers have to be replaced twice as often as shirts worn by female officers. Factors contributing to the wear and tear on men's shirts were: Too many wearings between washings, rough handling by commercial laundries, and rips and blood stains left after fights. Women's shirts lasted longer because they were changed daily, laundered at home by hand and carefully pressed, and because they were almost never torn or stained. Ms. Sunshine estimated that a department of nine hundred female officers and one hundred male officers would have to spend over $1,500 more a year on shirts alone than a department of one thousand female officers. It is important to note that although Ms. Sunshine's study had to do only with shirts, it has broad implications for all parts of the police uniform.

Cost of facilities would increase if police departments have to build separate locker rooms and rest rooms for male officers. Another additional cost would be incurred if new police call boxes had to be installed above the present ones to avoid the poor public image created by male police officers kneeling down to use the phone.

PERFORMANCE

A report just released by the City Institute gives the results of a study of the Soilington, D.C., police department, the first in the country to assign a substantial number of men to regular police duties. Policemen were involved in far more problems or incidents of serious misconduct than policewomen, ranging from traffic accidents to using a gun improperly. About 17 percent of the men in the study had misconduct listed in their departmental records, compared to 1 percent of the women. Twice as many men than women had been fired "in the best interests of the department."

The critical question is this: If we were willing to bear all the increased expense, adverse citizen reaction and discipline problems that putting men on patrol entails, would men be successful as patrol officers? Probably not. One prominent concern—aggressiveness—has received the most attention. There is abundant research to support the notion that men are more likely to show overt aggression against others when presented with interpersonal stress or threat. For example, Bandana and Walter (1969) in a quasi-experimental laboratory study found that male recruits were six times as likely as female recruits to punch out Bobo dolls after receiving critical feedback from superiors. Hilda Toker in her book *Violent Persons* reviews three decades of psychological research and concludes that men have been shown to be consistently more likely than women to act out psychopathic, homicidal, aggressive, blatant, latent and patent impulses. In short the research shows that before men could be allowed on patrol, there would have to be costly remedial training in nonassaultive and passive-aggressive techniques for handling interpersonal confrontations.

The City Institute staffers, who spent hundreds of hours observing men and women on patrol in Soilington, observed that when a prisoner resists arrest, men revert to caveman instincts and beat the prisoner with fists or clubs. Women, on the other hand, rely on psychology and sophisticated modern equipment such as mace to subdue the prisoner without inflicting injury. Dr. Willie Friedwoman of the Institute concluded that for each one hour of male street time, 4.6 more minutes of violent police-citizen interaction would occur if men continued to patrol than now occurs per hour of female street time. This figure would rise exponentially over time as citizens came to expect such treatment and to reciprocate in kind. Those results would generate lost-time increases for the following categories: giving aid to stricken victims, transporting police and citizens to medical facilities, court appearances in civil suits against officers and down time for officer disability. The cost figure of the introduction of patrolmen could be calculated by each department with the following simplified econometric model according to Dr. Friedwoman: $(n_1 + n_2)!/(n_1)(n_2)! \times T^2 + p(\cos n)^3$.

Another controversial issue is male sexuality as it affects performance and poses a serious threat to citizen welfare. The dominance of unbridled libidos in the potential male recruit raises the very real possibility of unseemly and offensive heterosexual behavior when possessed of the attributes of official sanction. Again a finding by Bandana and her colleagues is relevant. They found (*Journal of Primate Behavior*, 1968) that sailors were more likely than WAVES to make passes at scantily clad, life-size Bobo dolls of the opposite sex when placed conspicuously in their barracks. These tendencies could cause problems during stops and frisks, transports and follow-up interviews at homes of complainants.

Patty Block, evaluator of the pilot projects in Old York City and Soilington, D.C., noted that men exhibit a distinct deficiency when observing suspicious persons. She noted that male officers tended to keep females under observation although these persons are not generally associated with criminal activity. In particular Block has noted that there seemed to be a direct correlation between the chest size of the suspect and the length of observations. Researchers have been unable, however, to establish any correlation between chest size and criminality. Female officers, in contrast, keep their eyes on young, athletic, crime-prone males. Even if we were to assume that male officers may have stumbled on some as yet unrecognized criminal group, they strangely destroy all possible value of their observations by making peculiar whistling noises, thereby alerting the suspects.

Without dwelling on the sexuality problem too long, the point must be made that there could be embarrassments caused by allowing men to ride in patrol cars with policewomen on the midnight shift. Recently, husbands of policewomen in Old Orleans marched on police headquarters and caused so much commotion that the police department had to abandon its experiment of using men in patrol cars.

The blatant performance problems caused by male aggressiveness and sexuality must not be allowed to overshadow the subtler problems posed by men's deficiencies in social skills. The City Institute's multiphasic factor analytic studies in Old York City and Soilington, D.C., proved that women are more socially adept, emotionally responsive and gregarious than men. They possess superior skills in communication—written and oral. City Institute researchers found that these were the indispensable skills needed for the 90 percent service-oriented police calls.

MEN'S PLACE IN LAW ENFORCEMENT

The previous remarks are not intended to suggest that men have no place in law enforcement. On the contrary, men have some special qualities which are needed in police work. When riots or other uncontrollable fights break out suddenly and there is not time to gather sophisticated equipment, build barriers, or use other humane approaches to crowd control and apprehension of violent criminals, the police department needs the brute force that big men can best provide.

The question always arises, however, of what to do with the men between occurrences requiring their brute strength. One suggestion is that a few can be used in patrol wagons. Wagon drivers rarely handle the routine police calls for which men are considered unsuitable and they do frequently transport male prisoners who must be searched. The city of Los Diablos has just completed a year-long innovative demonstration project of assigning one man to each patrol wagon. Chief Edith Sivad reports that the project is an outstanding success! Time spent in having to call a policeman from across the city to search a male prisoner was almost completely eliminated. The men assigned to the wagons were even effective with some of the female prisoners. While the policewomen sometimes had to fight to get a woman into the wagon, the men could use their masculine wiles. Particularly with drunk women, the men could flirt with the woman and get her into the wagon before she knew what happened. (But hiring a police officer simply for his handsome face has its limitations.)

It is also possible to use one man in each of the station houses which have cell blocks so that a man would be available for searches there. More than one man per station, however, might decrease the efficiency of the clerical operations that must be performed. Although it must be acknowledged that the Bell Telephone Company has begun using men as telephone operators and clerks, police departments would be wise to await the results of that experiment before hiring too many men for such work in police departments.

Other rational suggestions for greater utilization of men include traffic control where their added height makes them more visible and where they have few citizen contacts; and in police athletic programs for teenage boys where the fact that they would be out of uniform reduces their tendencies toward authority and aggression problems.

In summary, research, experience and common sense dictate that men are not suited for the full range of police duties. It is felt that to introduce great numbers of men into police departments would seriously interfere with the efficiency of the broad police services now performed. However, a few carefully selected men can be used in special areas.

Appendix
National Directory of
Counseling Resources

The following individuals and organizations have indicated interest and experience in counseling women seeking redress for sex discrimination in employment. All of the resources listed have volunteered and many are unknown to the authors. Some are professionals in private practice (lawyers, psychologists) and may charge for professional services; a woman who approaches any of those listed should clearly inquire about this point before making any appointments for consultation. Others work for organizations which pay their salaries and thus, performing such services is a part of their jobs. Still others have filed an action personally or have assisted other women because of their commitment to equality in employment, and they are willing to devote their time without reimbursement.

If any readers contact an individual or organization for counseling during a sex discrimination action, we hope you will take the time to return to us the form provided for evaluation of these services. You are also invited to submit names and addresses of potential resources who have not been mentioned. In any future publications, we would like to be able to recommend individuals and organizations who can provide effective support to women during the critical days or weeks of the action.

If you yourself take action or if you assist another woman and call upon one of the people listed as resources, I hope that you will return the questionnaire to:

Virginia E. Pendergrass, Ph.D.
Social Work Program
Florida International University
Miami, FL 33199.

The individuals and organizations are coded in the list according to the types of experience they reported as follows:

A. This person has her/himself taken sex discrimination action.

B. This person has assisted women in
   1. planning strategy for an informal action
   2. pursuing a formal grievance
   3. filing with a government agency
   4. filing suit privately

C. This person has experience in sex discrimination as
   1. a lawyer
   2. a union representative
   3. an equal employment agency representative
   4. an affirmative-action officer

CODE

Arizona

A	Beverly Powell
B 1, 2, 3, 4	EEOC, Suite 1450
C 3	Valley Center
	201 North Central
	Phoenix 85253
	(602) 261-3882 - work
	(602) 994-3910 - home

Arkansas

C 3	Margaret Casinger
	21 Brooklawn Drive
	Little Rock 72205
	(501) 225-3373

Alabama

A	Dr. Kathleen P. Faircloth
B 1, 2	923 Saulter Road
	Birmingham 35209

B 1, 3   Virginia Sparks Volker
                  3424 Altamont Road
                  Birmingham   35205
                  (205) 323-4804 - home
                  (205) 934-3526 - work

California

B 1, 2, 3, 4   John F. Moulds, III
C 1   1007 Seventh Street
                  Sacramento   95814

B 1, 2   Doreen Seidler-Feller
                  933 South Hilgard Avenue
                  Apartment #303
                  Los Angeles   90024
                  (213) 478-6270

B 1   Jane Soltman
                  1376 Kelton Avenue
                  Los Angeles   90024
                  (215) 477-0712

B 1, 4   Michele Andrisin Wittig
C 4   Associate Professor of Psychology
                  California State University
                  Northridge   91324
                  (213) 885-2827

Colorado

B 1, 2, 4   Hannah J. Evans
                  831 14th Street
                  Denver   80202
                  (303) 629-0690

Connecticut

                  Angela H. Fichter
                  P.O. Box 1291
                  Burlington   06013

Florida

B 1, 2, 3, 4   Roberta Fulton Fox
C 1   Gold and Fox, P.A.
                  Attorneys at Law
                  4651 Ponce de Leon
                  Coral Gables   33146
                  (305) 667-2152

A   Ellen Kimmel, Ph.D.
B 1, 2, 3   College of Education
                      University of South Florida
                      Tampa   33620
                      (813) 974-2100

B 1   Frances Kramer
                      18101 N.W. Seventh Avenue
                      Miami   33179
                      (305) 652-7550

A   Margaret Y. Menzel, Ph.D.
B 3, 4   1605 Kolopakin Nene
C 2   Tallahassee 32301
                      (904) 877-1934

B 1, 2, 3   Ann S. Miller
C 3   7900 N.W. 45 Street
                      Lauderhill 33321
                      (305) 741-2568 - home
                      (305) 584-9540 - work

B 1, 2, 3   Claire F. Mitchel
C 3   Broward County
                         Human Relations Division
                      3521 West Broward Boulevard
                      Ft. Lauderdale 33312

B 1, 2   Dorothy Nevill, Ph.D.
C 4   Department of Psychology
                      University of Florida
                      Gainesville 32611
                      (904) 392-0617

A   Virginia E. Pendergrass, Ph.D.
B 1, 2, 3, 4   Social Work Program
                      Florida International University
                      Tamiami Trail
                      Miami   33199
                      (305) 552-2324

B 1   Joyce Peterson
C 2   3060 N.W. 15 Street
                      Miami   33125
                      (305) 635-3096

Georgia

A
B 1, 2, 3, 4

Martha W. Gaines
2444-E Adina Drive, N.E.
Atlanta   30324
(404) 261-1836

Illinois

A
B 1, 2, 3, 4
C 4

Norma W. Pendleton
7620 South Ingleside Avenue
Chicago   60619
(312) 483-1050

Iowa

A

Serena Stier, Ph.D.
302 Olde Hickory Ridge
Coralville   52241

Maine

A
B 1, 2, 3, 4
C 3

Terry Ann Lunt-Aucoin
Maine Human Rights Commission
State House
Augusta   04333
(207) 289-2326

B 3

Maine Civil Liberties Union
97 A Exchange Street
Portland   04111
(207) 774-5444

A
B 1, 3, 4

Lois Reckitt
38 Myrtle Avenue
South Portland   04106
(207) 799-8744

Massachusetts

A

9 to 5 Organization for
   Women Office Workers

B 1, 2, 3, 4

140 Clarendon Street
Boston   02116
(617) 536-6002

B 1, 2, 3, 4
C 2

Karen Nussbaum
Local 925
140 Clarendon Street
Boston   02116
(617) 267-0930

Minnesota

A	Kathy Olson
B 1, 4	192 Seymour Avenue, S.E.
	Minneapolis 55414
	(612) 333-6870

Montana

B 1, 2, 3, 4	Kathleen F. Holden
C 4	2713 South Hills Drive
	Missoula 59801
	(406) 549-2095

A	Maureen Fleming Ullrich, Ph.D.
B 1	School of Business Administration
	University of Montana
	Missoula 59801
	(406) 243-2273

Nevada

A	Catherine P. Smith
B 1, 3	1730 O'Farrell Street
	Reno 89503
	(702) 747-4560

New Hampshire

B 2, 3	Berel Firestone
C 3	66 South Street
	Concord 03301
	(603) 271-2761

B 1, 3, 4	Judi Hartwell
	111 Clark Road
	Rye 03870
	(603) 436-5758

B 1, 3	Susan Pelton
	Box 997
	Henniker 03242
	(603) 225-3080

New York

A	Renata Berg-Pan
B 1, 2, 4	143-36 Poplar Avenue
	Flushing 11355
	(212) 359-0970

A   Laura Fassio-Canuto
                52 Riverside Drive
                New York   10024
                (212) 799-3794

B 1, 2, 3, 4   Norman E. Henkin
C 1   50 Broadway
                New York 10004
                (212) 344-4200

A   Dr. Marguerite F. Levy
                241 Sackett Street
                Brooklyn   11231

A   Felicia Shpritzer, Lieutenant
                New York Police Department (retired)
                446 East 20 Street
                New York   10009
                (212) 228-4742

                          North Carolina

A   Ruth W. Nerboso
                Box 179
                Cullowhee   28723
                (704) 293-9375

B 1   Judith M. Stillion, Ph.D.
C 3   Western Carolina University
                Cullowhee   28723
                (704) 293-7247

                          North Dakota

A   Marcia Niemann
B 3   219 12th Street South
                Apartment No. 1
                Faye   58102
                (701) 293-7027

Ohio

A   Dorothy E. Thorne, M.S.S., A.C.S.W.
Department of Social Services
Cleveland State University
Cleveland 44155
(216) 687-4560

B 3, 4   Women's Law Fund, Inc.
C 1   1621 Euclid Avenue
Suite 620
Cleveland 44115

Pennsylvania

B 1, 2   Lancaster Women's Center
230 West Chestnut Street
Lancaster 17603
(717) 299-5381

B 1, 2, 3, 4   Gloria Sackman-Reed
P.O. Box 3457
Williamsport 17701
(717) 326-6567

Rhode Island

B 1, 3, 4   Angela H. Fichter
C 3   334 Westminster Mall
Providence 02903
(401) 277-2661 - work
215 Doyle Avenue
Providence 02906
(401) 861-0577 - home

A   Miriam Kapsinow
B 1, 4   18 Whitin Avenue
Warwick 02888

A   Jane K. Thompson
B 1, 3   14 Centennial Street
Warwick 02886
(401) 739-1269
(evenings and weekends)

South Carolina

A	Victoria L. Eslinger
B 1, 2, 3, 4	Eslinger & Knowles
C 1	Attorneys at Law
	1210 Pickens Street
	Columbia 29201
	(803) 771-8774

Virginia

A	Ruth M. Lunn, Psychologist
B 1, 2, 3, 4	1344 North Lynnbrook Drive
	Arlington 22201
	(703) 528-1706
	Box 174, Route 2
	Sterling 22170
	(703) 430-2487
	(see also Washington, D.C.)

Washington

A	Seattle NOW Employment
	Advocate Corps
B 1, 2, 3, 4	South Seattle NOW
C 1, 3	2252 Sixth-Fifth, N.W.
	Seattle
	(206) 523-2121

Washington, D.C.

A	Mary Ellen Abrecht
B 1	9 Eighth Street, N.E.
C 1	Washington, D.C.
	(202) 426-7165

A	Marcia Greenberger and Margy Kohn
B 1, 2, 3, 4	Women's Rights Project
C 1	Center for Law and Social Policy
	1751 N Street, N.W.
	Washington, D.C. 20036
	(202) 872-0670

A	Ruth M. Lunn, Psychologist
B 1, 2, 3, 4	1726 Eye Street, N.W.
	Suite 613
	Washington, D.C. 20006
	(202) 298-6629

B 1, 2, 3, 4   Women's Legal Defense Fund, Inc.
                  #210, 1010 Vermont Avenue, N.W.
                  Washington, D.C.   20005
                  (202) 638-1123-6

                       Wisconsin

B 1, 2, 3   Norma Briggs, Executive Director
C 3   Wisconsin Governor's Commission
                     on the Status of Women
                  30 West Mifflin Street, Rm. 210
                  Madison   53703
                  (608) 266-1162

C 1   Valerie S. Mannis
                  111 South Fairchild Street
                  Madison   53703
                  (608) 257-5126

A   Doris K. Schermer
B 1, 2, 3, 4   1621-K. West Edgerton Avenue
                  Milwaukee   53221
                  (414) 282-2486

B 1, 2, 3, 4   Gretchen T. Vetzner
C 1   302 East Washington, Suite 209
                  Madison   53703
                  (608) 255-9769

B 1, 2, 3, 4   Daphne Webb
C 1   222 South Hamilton Street,
                  Suite 22
                  Madison   53703
                  (608) 255-0107

Recommendation of Resource Person
or Organization

I would like the person(s)/organization(s) below to be included as a resource for women contemplating action to combat sex discrimination in employment:

Name _____

Address _____ Zip _____
            Street   City   State

Telephone: Area _____ Number _____

Name _____

Address _____ Zip _____
            Street   City   State

Telephone: Area _____ Number _____

* * * * * * * *

Evaluation of Resource Person
or Organization

I consulted with the person(s)/organization(s) listed below regarding an action combating sex discrimination in employment:

Name _____

Address _____ Zip _____
            Street   City   State

Telephone: Area _____ Number _____

The type of action I wished to initiate was
          _____ formal grievance within organization
          _____ union grievance
          _____ filing with a government agency
          _____ filing suit privately

Please give a brief statement of the problem involved

_____

_____

_____

_____

_____

After consultation, the action that I decided to take was
       _____ no action
       _____ informal persuasive action
       _____ formal grievance within organization
       _____ union grievance
       _____ filing with government agency
       _____ filing suit privately

If action was completed, please indicate outcome:
       _____ unsuccessful
       _____ successful

   Comment? _____

_____

_____

_____

_____

The type of support I *wanted* from the resource person/
organization was
       _____ planning strategy
       _____ personal support
       _____ legal advice
       _____ financial backing

The type of support I *received* was
_____ planning strategy
_____ personal support
_____ legal advice
_____ financial backing

The person/organization expected reimbursement as follows:
_____ no charge involved
_____ minimal charges necessitated by action
_____ reasonable professional fees and charges
_____ charges were very high
_____ I was refused consultation because I could not pay charges

If another woman asked me to refer her to a person/organization for advice regarding a sex discrimination in employment action, I would
_____ refer her to the person/organization who helped me, for the following types of support (check as many as apply)
_____ planning strategy
_____ personal support
_____ legal advice
_____ not refer her to the person/organization who helped me because _____

_____

_____

_____

_____

Other comments, if any _____

_____

_____

_____

Notes

Chapter 1: Introduction

1. M. Eastwood, *Fighting Job Discrimination: Three Federal Approaches* (Washington, D.C. 1971).

2. H.S. Astin, "Employment and Career Status of Women Psychologists," *American Psychologist* 27(1972):371-81.

3. H.S. Astin and A.E. Bayer, "Sex Discrimination in Academe," *Educational Record* 53(1972):101-18.

4. L.S. Fidell, "Empirical Verification of Sex Discrimination in Hiring Practices in Psychology," *American Psychologist* 25(1970):1094-98.

5. C.A. Boneau and J.M. Cuca, "An Overview of Psychology's Human Resources," *American Psychologist* 29(1974):821-40.

6. J. Cates, "Sex and Salary," *American Psychologist* 28(1973):929.

7. M. Teghtsoonian, "Distribution by Sex of Authors and Editors of Psychological Journals, 1970-72," *American Psychologist* 29(1974):262-69.

8. B. Piacente, "Women as Experimenters," *American Psychologist* 29(1974):536-39.

9. L. Guyer and L. Fidell, "Publications of Men and Women Psychologists," *American Psychologist* 28(1973):157-60.

10. V. Isambert-Jamati, "Absenteeism Among Women Workers in Industry," *International Labor Review* 85(1962):248-61.

11. E.B. Kimmel, "Status of Women in the Psychological Community in the Southeast: A Case Study," *American Psychologist* 29(1974):519-40.

12. R.J. Simon et al., "The Woman Ph.D.: A Recent Profile," *Social Problems* 15(1967):221-36.

13. M. Williams et al., "Career Patterns: More Grist for Women's Liberation," *Journal of National Association of Social Workers* 19(1974):463-66.

14. A. V. Adams, *Toward Fair Employment and the EEOC* (Washington, D.C.: U.S. Equal Employment Opportunity Commission, 1972).

15. Women's Bureau, *Handbook on Women Workers* (Washington, D.C.: U.S. Government Printing Office, 1969).

16. J.M. Kreps, "The Occupations: Wide Economic Opportunity," in M.L. McBee and K.A. Blake (eds.), *The American Woman: Who Will She Be?* (Beverly Hills, Cal.: Glencoe, 1974).

17. Women's Bureau, *Fact Sheet on the Earnings Gap* (Washington, D.C.: U.S. Government Printing Office, 1970).

18. "Affirmative Inaction on Campus: Will the Real Victims Stand Up?" *The Spokeswoman* 5(1974):5.

Chapter 2: Friendly Little Chats

1. A. Theodore, "Academic Women in Protest," unpublished manuscript, Simmons College, 1974.

2. *Ibid.*

3. A.M. Hacker, "Women as a Minority Group," *Social Forces* 30(1951):60-69.

4. M.A. Clifton and H.M. Smith, "Comparison of Expressed Self-Concepts of Highly Skilled Males and Females Concerning Motor Performance," *Perceptual and Motor Skills* 16(1963):199-201.

5. P. Goldberg, "Are Women Prejudiced Against Women?" *Transaction* 5(1968):28-31.

6. J.P. McKee and A.C. Sherrifs, "The Differential Evaluation of Males and Females," *Journal of Personality* 25(1957):356-71.

7. D. Copus et al., *A Unique Competence: A Study of Equal Employment Opportunity in the Bell System* (Washington, D.C.: U.S. Equal Employment Opportunity Commission, 1971).

8. C. Bird, *Born Female* (New York, Pocket Books, 1971).

9. Association of American Colleges Project on the Status and Education of Women, "Courts Issue Injunctions to Prohibit Institutions from Terminating Women Faculty Who Allege Discrimination," press release, Washington, D.C., 1974.

Chapter 5: Affirmative-Action Offices—How They Can and Cannot Help

1. S. Gemmell, *Affirmative Action Officers In Higher Education*, unpublished doctoral dissertation, Indiana University, 1974.

2. L.J. Weitzman, "Affirmative Action Plans for Eliminating Sex Discrimination in Academe," in A.S. Rossi and A. Calderwood (eds.), *Academic Women on the Move* (New York: Russell Sage Foundation, 1973).

3. Gemmell.

4. G.C. Christensen, Letter to the Council on Academic Affairs of the National Association of State Universities and Land Grant Colleges, Iowa University, October 15, 1973.

5. *Affirmative Action Plan for Equal Employment Opportunity* (revised supplement), University of Florida, January 1975.

6. *The Spokeswoman*, July 15, August 15 and November 15, 1974; January 15, 1975.

7. R.L. Hurst, "Qualitative Variables in Regression Analysis," *American Educational Research Journal* 7(1970):541-52.

8. N.M. Gordon et al., "Faculty Salaries: Is There Discrimination by Sex, Race, and Discipline?" *American Economic Review* 64(1974):419-27.

9. B.B. Reagan and B.J. Maynard, "Sex Discrimination in Universities: An Approach through Internal Labor Market Analysis," *AAUP Bulletin* 60(1974):13-21.

10. A.E. Bayer and H.S. Astin, "Sex Differentials in the Academic Reward System," *Science* 188(1975):796-802.

11. Weitzman.

12. I. Thompson, *Summary of Counterparting Procedures,* Report to the Office of Academic Affairs, University of Florida, May 1973.

Chapter 7: The Local Civil Rights Agency
1. E.M. Gould, *American Woman Today* (Englewood Cliffs, N.J.: Prentice-Halll, Inc., 1972).

2. S. Hybels and R.L. Weaver, *Speech Communication* (New York: Van Nostrand, 1974), 181-216.

3. Gould.

4. National Council of Negro Women, Inc., *Women and Housing: A Report on Sex Discrimination in Five American Cities* (Washington, D.C.: U.S. Department of Housing and Urban Development, 1975).

5. *Summary of Relationships Between EECC and State and Local Anti-Discrimination Agencies* (Atlanta, Ga.: Equal Employment Opportunity Commission, 1976).

6. E.K. Paschall and E.G. Turlington, *Because of Sex: A Handbook on Sex Discrimination in Employment* (Atlanta, Ga.: Feminist Committee Press, 1975).

7. R.E. Smith, "To the President, the Equal Employment Opportunity Commission and How to Make It Work," *Ms. Magazine* 8(1976):62ff.

8. *A Guide to Affirmative Action in Employment* (second

revision) (Ft. Lauderdale, Fla.: Broward County Community Relations Commission, 1974).

9. D. Jongeward and D. Scott, *Affirmative Action for Women: A Practical Guide* (Reading, Mass.: Addison-Wesley, 1975).

Chapter 9: Academic Women and Unions

1. V. Mulrooney, "Women in Higher Education," AFT Conference on Women in Higher Education, May 1973.

2. J. Kitch, "AFT Negotiates Change for College Women," pamphlet prepared by American Federation of Teachers College Universities department, n.d.

3. E. Raphael, "Working Women and Their Membership in Labor Unions," *Monthly Labor Review* 97(1974):27-33.

4. R. Dorr, "Education and Women's Rights: What the Law Now Says," *American Education* 8(1972):4-10.

5. S. Tobias, "Affirmative Action for Women in the Universities: Why All the Fuss?" *Radcliffe Quarterly* 60(1974):14-16.

6. A.H. Cook, "Women and Trade Unions," *Annals of the American Academy of Political and Social Science* 375(1968): 124-32.

7. L.M. Dowey, "Women in Labor Unions," *Monthly Labor Review* 94(1971):42-48.

Chapter 11: Filing a Sex Discrimination Charge with a Federal Agency

1. U.S. Department of Labor, *Equal Pay for Equal Work Under the Fair Labor Standards Act* (Washington, D.C.: U.S. Government Printing Office, 1971).

2. U.S. Department of Labor, *Equal Pay* (Washington, D.C.: U.S. Government Printing Office, 1974).

3. U.S. Department of Labor, *Handy Reference Guide to the Fair Labor Standards Act* (Washington, D.C.: U.S. Government Printing Office, 1975).

4. M. Eastwood, *Fighting Job Discrimination: Three Federal Approaches* (Washington, D.C.: Today Publications, 1971).

5. Labor Law Reports, "New 1972 Equal Employment Opportunity Law with Explanation," *Labor Law Reports* 293(1972):1-71.

6. S.C. Ross, *The Rights of Women* (New York: Avon, 1973).

Chapter 13: Legal Suits

1. S.D. Ross, *The Rights of Women* (New York: Avon, 1973).

2. M. Eastwood, *Fighting Job Discrimination: Three Federal Approaches* (Washington, D..C.: Today Publications, 1971).

3. K. Grimstad and S. Rennie (eds.), *The New Woman's Survival Catalog* (New York: Coward, McCann and Geoghegan, 1973).

4. B. Sandler, *Federal Laws and Regulations Concerning Race and Sex Discrimination in Educational Institutions* (Washington, D.C.: Association of American Colleges, 1973).

5. *Ibid.*

Chapter 15: Sex Discrimination: Special Problems of Black Women

1. C.C. Killingworth, *Jobs and Income for Negroes* (Washington, D.C.: U.S. Government Printing Office, 1968).

2. U.S. Bureau of Census, *Population Reports* (Washington, D.C.: U.S. Government Printing Office, 1960).

3. A. Lincoln, "Who Will Reverse the Black Woman," in T. Caade (ed.), *The Black Woman* (New York: American Library, 1970).

4. P. Rena Marshall, in T. Cade (ed.), *The Black Woman* (New York: American Library, 1970).

5. "At Home, Fred's a Nice, Nice Guy," *Ebony Magazine* 30(1975):53.

6. F.M. Beal, "Double Jeopardy: To Be Black and Female," in R. Morgon (ed.), *Sisterhood is Powerful* (New York: Random House, 1970).

7. Black Women's Liberation Group, "Statement on Birth Control," in R. Morgon (ed.), *Sisterhood is Powerful* (New York: Random House, 1970).

8. P.G. Fulcher et al., *Report on the Task Force on Minority Women and Women's Rights* (Chicago, Ill.: National Organization for Women, 1974).

9. F.S. Foster, "Changing Concepts of Black Women," *Journal of Black Studies* 3(1973):433-54.

10. A. Theodore, "Academic Women in Protest," unpublished manuscript, Simmons College, 1974.

Chapter 17: Personal Counseling During Sex Discrimination
Actions

1. E. Janeway, *Man's World, Woman's Place* (New York: Delta, 1971), 119-33.

2. A. Theodore, "Academic Women in Protest," unpublished manuscript, Simmons College, 1974.

3. C.M. Nadelson, "Adjustment: New Approaches to Women's Mental Health," in M.L. McBee and R.A. Blake (eds.), *The American Woman: Who Will She Be?* (Beverly Hills, Cal.: Glencoe Press, 1974).

4. J. Agel (ed.), *The Radical Therapist* (New York: Ballantine, 1971).

5. J. Agel (ed.), *Rough Times* (New York: Ballantine, 1973).

6. A. Theodore.

7. C. Bird, *Everything a Woman Needs to Know to Get Paid What She's Worth* (New York: David McKay, 1973).

8. A. Theodore.

9. R. Loring and T. Wells, *Breakthrough: Women Into Management* (New York: Van Nostrand, 1972).

10. J. Bardwick, *Psychology of Women* (New York: Harper and Row, 1971).

11. M.S. Horner, "Fail: Bright Women," *Psychology Today* 3(1969):36.

12. A. Steinman, "Cultural Values, Female Role Expectancies and Therapeutic Goals: Research and Interpretation," in V. Franks and V. Burtle (eds.), *Women in Therapy* (New York: Brunner/Mazel, 1974).

13. S. Phelps and A. Austin, *The Assertive Woman* (San Luis Obispo, Cal.: Impact Press, 1975).

14. L.Z. Bloom et al., *The New Assertive Woman* (New York: Delacorte Press, 1975).

15. C.F. Epstein, *Woman's Place* (Berkeley: University of California Press, 1970).

16. Women in Transition, Inc., *Women in Transition* (New York: Scribner's, 1975).

Chapter 18: Men's Work: Women in Criminal Justice

1. F. Shpritzer, "Case for the Promotion of Policewomen in the City of New York," *Journal of Criminology and Police Science* 50(1959):415–19.

2. *Shpritzer v. Lang*, 234 N.Y.S. 2d 285 (1962).

3. C.H. Milton, *Women in Policing, A Manual* (Washington, D.C.: Police Foundation, 1974).

4. B. Price, *A Study of Leadership Strength of Female Police Executives*, Law Enforcement and Correction Services, Pennsylvania State University, University Park, December 1973.

5. C. Milton, *Women in Policing* (Washington, D.C.: Police Foundation, 1972).

6. P.B. Bloch and D. Anderson, *Policewomen on Patrol, Final Report* (Washington, D.C.: Police Foundation, 1974).

7. International Association of Chiefs of Police, *Police Selection Survey* (Washington, D.C., 1971).

8. J.V. Wilson, Police Report, *A View of Law Enforcement* (Boston, Mass.: Little, Brown and Company, 1975).

9. 38 C.F.R. 6115 (1973).

10. *Smith v. Troyan*, 520 F. 2d 492 (6th cir. 1975).

11. T.W. White and P.B. Bloch, *Police Officer Height and Selected Aspects of Performance* (Washington, D.C.: Police Foundation, 1975).

12. *Mieth v. Dothard*, 418 F. Supp. 1169 (M.D. Ala. 1976).

13. C.H. Milton.

14. *Schaeffer v. Tanian*, 394 F. Supp. 1128 (E.D. Mich. 1974).

15. *United States v. City of Chicago*, 411 F. Supp. (N.D. Ill. 1976) and 385 F. Supp. 543 (N.D. Ill. 1974).

16. *Roller v. City of San Mateo*, 406 F. Supp. 362 (N.D. Cal. 1975).

17. *Officers for Justice v. Civil Service Commission*, 395 F. Supp. 378 (N.D. Cal. 1975).

18.[1] P.B. Bloch and D. Anderson.

19. M.E. Abrecht, *The Making of a Woman Cop* (New York: Wm. R. Morrow, Inc., 1976).

20. A. Fleming, *New on the Beat: Women in the Police Force* (New York: Coward, McCann and Geoghegan, 1976).

Index

INVENTORY 1983